FREE Test Taking Tips Video/DVD Offer

To better serve you, we created videos covering test taking tips that we want to give you for FREE. **These videos cover world-class tips that will help you succeed on your test.**

We just ask that you send us feedback about this product. Please let us know what you thought about it—whether good, bad, or indifferent.

To get your **FREE videos**, you can use the QR code below or email freevideos@studyguideteam.com with "Free Videos" in the subject line and the following information in the body of the email:

    a. The title of your product

    b. Your product rating on a scale of 1-5, with 5 being the highest

    c. Your feedback about the product

If you have any questions or concerns, please don't hesitate to contact us at info@studyguideteam.com.

Thank you!

GMAT Prep Book 2025-2026
2 Practice Tests and Study Guide for GMAT Focus
[10th Edition]

Lydia Morrison

Copyright © 2025 by TPB Publishing

All rights reserved. No part of this publication may be reproduced, distributed, or transmitted in any form or by any means, including photocopying, recording, or other electronic or mechanical methods, without the prior written permission of the publisher, except in the case of brief quotations embodied in critical reviews and certain other noncommercial uses permitted by copyright law.

Written and edited by TPB Publishing.

TPB Publishing is not associated with or endorsed by any official testing organization. TPB Publishing is a publisher of unofficial educational products. All test and organization names are trademarks of their respective owners. Content in this book is included for utilitarian purposes only and does not constitute an endorsement by TPB Publishing of any particular point of view.

Interested in buying more than 10 copies of our product? Contact us about bulk discounts:
bulkorders@studyguideteam.com

ISBN 13: 9781637757819

Table of Contents

Welcome 1
   FREE Videos/DVD OFFER 1

Quick Overview 2

Test-Taking Strategies 3

Introduction to the GMAT Focus Edition 7

Study Prep Plan for the GMAT Focus Edition 9

Quantitative Reasoning 10
   Arithmetic and Algebra 10
   Problem Solving 26
   Practice Quiz 27
   Answer Explanations 28

Verbal Reasoning 29
   Reading Comprehension 29
   Critical Reasoning 34
   Practice Quiz 38
   Answer Explanations 41

Data Insights 43
   Data Sufficiency 43
   Graphics Interpretation 44
   Multi-Source Reasoning 49
   Two-Part Analysis 53
   Table Analysis 54
   Practice Quiz 55

Answer Explanations 59

GMAT Practice Test #1 61
Quantitative Reasoning 61
Verbal Reasoning 66
Data Insights 75

Answer Explanations #1 89
Quantitative Reasoning 89
Verbal Reasoning 93
Data Insights 98

Practice Test #2 105
Quantitative Reasoning 105
Verbal Reasoning 109
Data Insights 118

Answer Explanations #2 131
Quantitative Reasoning 131
Verbal Reasoning 135
Data Insights 141

Index 147

Welcome

Dear Reader,

Welcome to your new Test Prep Books study guide! We are pleased that you chose us to help you prepare for your exam. There are many study options to choose from, and we appreciate you choosing us. Studying can be a daunting task, but we have designed a smart, effective study guide to help prepare you for what lies ahead.

Whether you're a parent helping your child learn and grow, a high school student working hard to get into your dream college, or a nursing student studying for a complex exam, we want to help give you the tools you need to succeed. We hope this study guide gives you the skills and the confidence to thrive, and we can't thank you enough for allowing us to be part of your journey.

In an effort to continue to improve our products, we welcome feedback from our customers. We look forward to hearing from you. Suggestions, success stories, and criticisms can all be communicated by emailing us at info@studyguideteam.com.

Sincerely,
Test Prep Books Team

FREE Videos/DVD OFFER

Doing well on your exam requires both knowing the test content and understanding how to use that knowledge to do well on the test. We offer completely FREE test taking tip videos. **These videos cover world-class tips that you can use to succeed on your test.**

To get your **FREE videos**, you can use the QR code below or email freevideos@studyguideteam.com with "Free Videos" in the subject line and the following information in the body of the email:

    a. The title of your product
    b. Your product rating on a scale of 1-5, with 5 being the highest
    c. Your feedback about the product
If you have any questions or concerns, please don't hesitate to contact us at info@studyguideteam.com.

Quick Overview

As you draw closer to taking your exam, effective preparation becomes more and more important. Thankfully, you have this study guide to help you get ready. Use this guide to help keep your studying on track and refer to it often.

This study guide contains several key sections that will help you be successful on your exam. The guide contains tips for what you should do the night before and the day of the test. Also included are test-taking tips. Knowing the right information is not always enough. Many well-prepared test takers struggle with exams. These tips will help equip you to accurately read, assess, and answer test questions.

A large part of the guide is devoted to showing you what content to expect on the exam and to helping you better understand that content. In this guide are practice test questions so that you can see how well you have grasped the content. Then, answer explanations are provided so that you can understand why you missed certain questions.

Don't try to cram the night before you take your exam. This is not a wise strategy for a few reasons. First, your retention of the information will be low. Your time would be better used by reviewing information you already know rather than trying to learn a lot of new information. Second, you will likely become stressed as you try to gain a large amount of knowledge in a short amount of time. Third, you will be depriving yourself of sleep. So be sure to go to bed at a reasonable time the night before. Being well-rested helps you focus and remain calm.

Be sure to eat a substantial breakfast the morning of the exam. If you are taking the exam in the afternoon, be sure to have a good lunch as well. Being hungry is distracting and can make it difficult to focus. You have hopefully spent lots of time preparing for the exam. Don't let an empty stomach get in the way of success!

When travelling to the testing center, leave earlier than needed. That way, you have a buffer in case you experience any delays. This will help you remain calm and will keep you from missing your appointment time at the testing center.

Be sure to pace yourself during the exam. Don't try to rush through the exam. There is no need to risk performing poorly on the exam just so you can leave the testing center early. Allow yourself to use all of the allotted time if needed.

Remain positive while taking the exam even if you feel like you are performing poorly. Thinking about the content you should have mastered will not help you perform better on the exam.

Once the exam is complete, take some time to relax. Even if you feel that you need to take the exam again, you will be well served by some down time before you begin studying again. It's often easier to convince yourself to study if you know that it will come with a reward!

Test-Taking Strategies

1. Predicting the Answer

When you feel confident in your preparation for a multiple-choice test, try predicting the answer before reading the answer choices. This is especially useful on questions that test objective factual knowledge. By predicting the answer before reading the available choices, you eliminate the possibility that you will be distracted or led astray by an incorrect answer choice. You will feel more confident in your selection if you read the question, predict the answer, and then find your prediction among the answer choices. After using this strategy, be sure to still read all of the answer choices carefully and completely. If you feel unprepared, you should not attempt to predict the answers. This would be a waste of time and an opportunity for your mind to wander in the wrong direction.

2. Reading the Whole Question

Too often, test takers scan a multiple-choice question, recognize a few familiar words, and immediately jump to the answer choices. Test authors are aware of this common impatience, and they will sometimes prey upon it. For instance, a test author might subtly turn the question into a negative, or he or she might redirect the focus of the question right at the end. The only way to avoid falling into these traps is to read the entirety of the question carefully before reading the answer choices.

3. Looking for Wrong Answers

Long and complicated multiple-choice questions can be intimidating. One way to simplify a difficult multiple-choice question is to eliminate all of the answer choices that are clearly wrong. In most sets of answers, there will be at least one selection that can be dismissed right away. If the test is administered on paper, the test taker could draw a line through it to indicate that it may be ignored; otherwise, the test taker will have to perform this operation mentally or on scratch paper. In either case, once the obviously incorrect answers have been eliminated, the remaining choices may be considered. Sometimes identifying the clearly wrong answers will give the test taker some information about the correct answer. For instance, if one of the remaining answer choices is a direct opposite of one of the eliminated answer choices, it may well be the correct answer. The opposite of obviously wrong is obviously right! Of course, this is not always the case. Some answers are obviously incorrect simply because they are irrelevant to the question being asked. Still, identifying and eliminating some incorrect answer choices is a good way to simplify a multiple-choice question.

4. Don't Overanalyze

Anxious test takers often overanalyze questions. When you are nervous, your brain will often run wild, causing you to make associations and discover clues that don't actually exist. If you feel that this may be a problem for you, do whatever you can to slow down during the test. Try taking a deep breath or counting to ten. As you read and consider the question, restrict yourself to the particular words used by the author. Avoid thought tangents about what the author *really* meant, or what he or she was *trying* to say. The only things that matter on a multiple-choice test are the words that are actually in the question. You must avoid reading too much into a multiple-choice question, or supposing that the writer meant

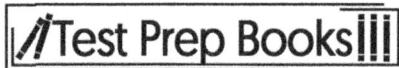

something other than what he or she wrote.

5. No Need for Panic

It is wise to learn as many strategies as possible before taking a multiple-choice test, but it is likely that you will come across a few questions for which you simply don't know the answer. In this situation, avoid panicking. Because most multiple-choice tests include dozens of questions, the relative value of a single wrong answer is small. As much as possible, you should compartmentalize each question on a multiple-choice test. In other words, you should not allow your feelings about one question to affect your success on the others. When you find a question that you either don't understand or don't know how to answer, just take a deep breath and do your best. Read the entire question slowly and carefully. Try rephrasing the question a couple of different ways. Then, read all of the answer choices carefully. After eliminating obviously wrong answers, make a selection and move on to the next question.

6. Confusing Answer Choices

When working on a difficult multiple-choice question, there may be a tendency to focus on the answer choices that are the easiest to understand. Many people, whether consciously or not, gravitate to the answer choices that require the least concentration, knowledge, and memory. This is a mistake. When you come across an answer choice that is confusing, you should give it extra attention. A question might be confusing because you do not know the subject matter to which it refers. If this is the case, don't

eliminate the answer before you have affirmatively settled on another. When you come across an answer choice of this type, set it aside as you look at the remaining choices. If you can confidently assert that one of the other choices is correct, you can leave the confusing answer aside. Otherwise, you will need to take a moment to try to better understand the confusing answer choice. Rephrasing is one way to tease out the sense of a confusing answer choice.

7. Your First Instinct

Many people struggle with multiple-choice tests because they overthink the questions. If you have studied sufficiently for the test, you should be prepared to trust your first instinct once you have carefully and completely read the question and all of the answer choices. There is a great deal of research suggesting that the mind can come to the correct conclusion very quickly once it has obtained all of the relevant information. At times, it may seem to you as if your intuition is working faster even than your reasoning mind. This may in fact be true. The knowledge you obtain while studying may be retrieved from your subconscious before you have a chance to work out the associations that support it. Verify your instinct by working out the reasons that it should be trusted.

8. Key Words

Many test takers struggle with multiple-choice questions because they have poor reading comprehension skills. Quickly reading and understanding a multiple-choice question requires a mixture of skill and experience. To help with this, try jotting down a few key words and phrases on a piece of scrap paper. Doing this concentrates the process of reading and forces the mind to weigh the relative importance of the question's parts. In selecting words and phrases to write down, the test taker thinks about the question more deeply and carefully. This is especially true for multiple-choice questions that are preceded by a long prompt.

9. Subtle Negatives

One of the oldest tricks in the multiple-choice test writer's book is to subtly reverse the meaning of a question with a word like *not* or *except*. If you are not paying attention to each word in the question, you can easily be led astray by this trick. For instance, a common question format is, "Which of the following is…?" Obviously, if the question instead is, "Which of the following is not…?," then the answer will be quite different. Even worse, the test makers are aware of the potential for this mistake and will include one answer choice that would be correct if the question were not negated or reversed. A test taker who misses the reversal will find what he or she believes to be a correct answer and will be so confident that he or she will fail to reread the question and discover the original error. The only way to avoid this is to practice a wide variety of multiple-choice questions and to pay close attention to each and every word.

10. Reading Every Answer Choice

It may seem obvious, but you should always read every one of the answer choices! Too many test takers fall into the habit of scanning the question and assuming that they understand the question because they recognize a few key words. From there, they pick the first answer choice that answers the question they believe they have read. Test takers who read all of the answer choices might discover that one of the latter answer choices is actually *more* correct. Moreover, reading all of the answer choices can remind you of facts related to the question that can help you arrive at the correct answer. Sometimes, a misstatement or incorrect detail in one of the latter answer choices will trigger your memory of the subject and will enable you to find the right answer. Failing to read all of the answer choices is like not reading all of the items on a restaurant menu: you might miss out on the perfect choice.

11. Spot the Hedges

One of the keys to success on multiple-choice tests is paying close attention to every word. This is never truer than with words like *almost*, *most*, *some*, and *sometimes*. These words are called "hedges" because they indicate that a statement is not totally true or not true in every place and time. An absolute statement will contain no hedges, but in many subjects, the answers are not always straightforward or absolute. There are always exceptions to the rules in these subjects. For this reason,

you should favor those multiple-choice questions that contain hedging language. The presence of qualifying words indicates that the author is taking special care with his or her words, which is certainly important when composing the right answer. After all, there are many ways to be wrong, but there is only one way to be right! For this reason, it is wise to avoid answers that are absolute when taking a multiple-choice test. An absolute answer is one that says things are either all one way or all another. They often include words like *every*, *always*, *best*, and *never*. If you are taking a multiple-choice test in a subject that doesn't lend itself to absolute answers, be on your guard if you see any of these words.

12. Long Answers

In many subject areas, the answers are not simple. As already mentioned, the right answer often requires hedges. Another common feature of the answers to a complex or subjective question are qualifying clauses, which are groups of words that subtly modify the meaning of the sentence. If the question or answer choice describes a rule to which there are exceptions or the subject matter is complicated, ambiguous, or confusing, the correct answer will require many words in order to be expressed clearly and accurately. In essence, you should not be deterred by answer choices that seem excessively long. Oftentimes, the author of the text will not be able to write the correct answer without offering some qualifications and modifications. Your job is to read the answer choices thoroughly and completely and to select the one that most accurately and precisely answers the question.

13. Restating to Understand

Sometimes, a question on a multiple-choice test is difficult not because of what it asks but because of how it is written. If this is the case, restate the question or answer choice in different words. This process serves a couple of important purposes. First, it forces you to concentrate on the core of the question. In order to rephrase the question accurately, you have to understand it well. Rephrasing the question will concentrate your mind on the key words and ideas. Second, it will present the information to your mind in a fresh way. This process may trigger your memory and render some useful scrap of information picked up while studying.

14. True Statements

Sometimes an answer choice will be true in itself, but it does not answer the question. This is one of the main reasons why it is essential to read the question carefully and completely before proceeding to the answer choices. Too often, test takers skip ahead to the answer choices and look for true statements. Having found one of these, they are content to select it without reference to the question above. The savvy test taker will always read the entire question before turning to the answer choices. Then, having settled on a correct answer choice, he or she will refer to the original question and ensure that the selected answer is relevant. The mistake of choosing a correct-but-irrelevant answer choice is especially common on questions related to specific pieces of objective knowledge.

15. No Patterns

One of the more dangerous ideas that circulates about multiple-choice tests is that the correct answers tend to fall into patterns. These erroneous ideas range from a belief that B and C are the most common right answers, to the idea that an unprepared test-taker should answer "A-B-A-C-A-D-A-B-A." It cannot be emphasized enough that pattern-seeking of this type is exactly the WRONG way to approach a multiple-choice test. To begin with, it is highly unlikely that the test maker will plot the correct answers according to some predetermined pattern. The questions are scrambled and delivered in a random order. Furthermore, even if the test maker was following a pattern in the assignation of correct answers, there is no reason why the test taker would know which pattern he or she was using. Any attempt to discern a pattern in the answer choices is a waste of time and a distraction from the real work of taking the test. A test taker would be much better served by extra preparation before the test than by reliance on a pattern in the answers.

Introduction to the GMAT Focus Edition

Function of the Test

The Graduate Management Admission Test (GMAT) Focus Edition, administered by the Graduate Management Admissions Council (GMAC), is the standard business school admissions exam in the United States. More than 2,100 business schools use the GMAT Focus Edition as part of their admissions criteria for MBA programs as well as other business-related programs like accounting and finance. The test is also used in admissions offices at some business schools around the world. The GMAT Focus Edition is not the only business school admissions test—an increasing number of schools accept GRE scores also or instead—but it remains the most common in the United States.

Approximately 300,000 people take the GMAT Focus Edition every year, although that total varies with the economy and other factors. Although business school admissions departments do consider a variety of factors in making decisions about prospective students, the GMAT Focus Edition score is typically the primary consideration and the most commonly discussed factor.

Test Administration

The GMAT Focus Edition is offered at approximately 600 testing centers in over 100 countries. It is offered year-round, and prospective test takers should either register for the GMAT Focus Edition at mba.com or make an appointment at a time that the test is offered at their preferred location. Upon completion of the exam, test takers can expect to receive their official score reports within 3-5 days. Then, after receiving their scores, test takers can choose to send a free score report to up to five schools.

Each section of the GMAT Focus Edition is made up of computer adaptive tests (CATs), meaning that they are given by computer and that the difficulty of questions offered to the test taker adapts to the test taker's performance up to that point. A unique feature of the GMAT Focus Edition is that test takers can review and edit the answers to the questions in each section before moving on. They will have the opportunity to do this from the Question Review & Edit screen, which appears at the end of each section. Test takers may review as many questions as they would like, but they may only edit up to three answers. Test takers can also bookmark questions as they move throughout the test, allowing an easy return to them from the Question Review & Edit screen.

Individuals are allowed to retake the GMAT Focus Edition as often as they wish, but not more than five times in one twelve-month period, or more than eight times in their life. Reasonable accommodations are available for test takers with disabilities in keeping with the Americans with Disabilities Act.

Test Format

The GMAT Focus Edition is 2 hours and 15 minutes long and includes 64 questions across three sections. There is also an optional 10-minute break. The three sections of the GMAT Focus Edition are Quantitative Reasoning, Verbal Reasoning, and Data Insights. Test takers may complete the test in any section order, and they may take the optional break after any section.

The Quantitative Reasoning section contains twenty-one problem solving questions covering arithmetic and algebra. You cannot use a calculator for this section. The Verbal Reasoning section is intended to measure the test taker's reading comprehension, critical thinking, and problem-solving skills. It contains twenty-three Reading Comprehension and Critical Reasoning questions. The Data Insights section of the GMAT Focus Edition tests for data literacy skills, including the test takers' ability to analyze data and apply it to real-life situations. It contains twenty questions that require test takers to use their data analysis, verbal reasoning, and math skills to solve. There will be an on-screen calculator provided for this section.

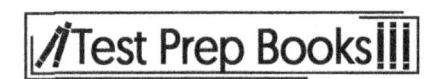

A summary of the sections of the GMAT Focus Edition is as follows:

Section	Questions	Time
Quantitative Reasoning	21 questions	45 minutes
Verbal Reasoning	23 questions	45 minutes
Data Insights	20 questions	45 minutes

Scoring

The GMAT Focus Edition score that test takers can choose to report to schools is a scaled score ranging from 205 to 805 reflecting the test taker's combined performance on all three sections of the exam. The average score of all test takers is usually around 540, and the standard deviation of all scores is 90 points, meaning that just over two-thirds of test takers fall in a range from 450 to 630. Top schools such as Harvard and Stanford admit students with average scores of around 700.

GMAT Focus Edition scores are based on the number of correct answers, with no penalty for guessing other than the missed opportunity to provide another correct response.

Study Prep Plan for the GMAT Focus Edition

1 **Schedule** - Use one of our study schedules below or come up with one of your own.

2 **Relax** - Test anxiety can hurt even the best students. There are many ways to reduce stress. Find the one that works best for you.

3 **Execute** - Once you have a good plan in place, be sure to stick to it.

One Week Study Schedule

Day 1	Quantitative Reasoning
Day 2	Verbal Reasoning
Day 3	Data Insights
Day 4	Practice Test #1
Day 5	Answer Explanations #1
Day 6	Practice Test #2
Day 7	Take Your Exam!

Two Week Study Schedule

Day 1	Quantitative Reasoning	Day 8	Recognizing Relationships in the Information
Day 2	Algebra	Day 9	Multi-Source Reasoning
Day 3	Problem Solving	Day 10	Practice Test #1
Day 4	Verbal Reasoning	Day 11	Answer Explanations #1
Day 5	Main Ideas and Supporting Details	Day 12	Practice Test #2
Day 6	Critical Reasoning	Day 13	Answer Explanations #2
Day 7	Data Insights	Day 14	Take Your Exam!

Build your own prep plan by visiting:
testprepbooks.com/prep

Quantitative Reasoning

Arithmetic and Algebra

Arithmetic

Addition with Whole Numbers and Fractions

Addition combines two quantities together. With whole numbers, this is taking two sets of things and merging them into one, then counting the result. For example, $4 + 3 = 7$. When adding numbers, the order does not matter: $3 + 4 = 7$, also. Longer lists of whole numbers can also be added together. The result of adding numbers is called the **sum**.

With fractions, the number on top is the **numerator**, and the number on the bottom is the **denominator**. To add fractions, the denominator must be the same—a **common denominator**. To find a common denominator, the existing numbers on the bottom must be considered, and the lowest number they will both multiply into must be determined. Consider the following equation:

$$\frac{1}{3} + \frac{5}{6} = ?$$

The numbers 3 and 6 both multiply into 6. Three can be multiplied by 2, and 6 can be multiplied by 1. The top and bottom of each fraction must be multiplied by the same number. Then, the numerators are added together to get a new numerator. The following equation is the result:

$$\frac{1}{3} + \frac{5}{6} = \frac{2}{6} + \frac{5}{6} = \frac{7}{6}$$

Subtraction with Whole Numbers and Fractions

Subtraction is taking one quantity away from another, so it is the opposite of addition. The expression $4 - 3$ means taking 3 away from 4. So, $4 - 3 = 1$. In this case, the order matters, since it entails taking one quantity away from the other, rather than just putting two quantities together. The result of subtraction is also called the **difference**.

To subtract fractions, the denominator must be the same. Then, subtract the numerators together to get a new numerator. Here is an example:

$$\frac{1}{3} - \frac{5}{6} = \frac{2}{6} - \frac{5}{6} = \frac{-3}{6} = -\frac{1}{2}$$

Multiplication with Whole Numbers and Fractions

Multiplication is a kind of repeated addition. The expression 4×5 is taking four sets, each of them having five things in them, and putting them all together. That means:

$$4 \times 5 = 5 + 5 + 5 + 5 = 20$$

As with addition, the order of the numbers does not matter. The result of a multiplication problem is called the **product**.

Quantitative Reasoning

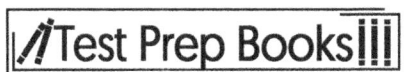

To multiply fractions, the numerators are multiplied to get the new numerator, and the denominators are multiplied to get the new denominator:

$$\frac{1}{3} \times \frac{5}{6} = \frac{1 \times 5}{3 \times 6} = \frac{5}{18}$$

When multiplying fractions, common factors can **cancel** or **divide into one another**, when factors that appear in the numerator of one fraction and the denominator of the other fraction. Here is an example:

$$\frac{1}{3} \times \frac{9}{8} = \frac{1}{1} \times \frac{3}{8}$$

$$1 \times \frac{3}{8} = \frac{3}{8}$$

The numbers 3 and 9 have a common factor of 3, so that factor can be divided out.

Division with Whole Numbers and Fractions

Division is the opposite of multiplication. With whole numbers, it means splitting up one number into sets of equal size. For example, $16 \div 8$ is the number of sets of eight things that can be made out of sixteen things. Thus, $16 \div 8 = 2$. As with subtraction, the order of the numbers will make a difference, here. The answer to a division problem is called the **quotient**, while the number in front of the division sign is called the **dividend**, and the number behind the division sign is called the **divisor**.

To divide fractions, the first fraction must be multiplied with the reciprocal of the second fraction. The **reciprocal** of the fraction $\frac{x}{y}$ is the fraction $\frac{y}{x}$. Here is an example:

$$\frac{1}{3} \div \frac{5}{6} = \frac{1}{3} \times \frac{6}{5} = \frac{6}{15} = \frac{2}{5}$$

Recognizing Equivalent Fractions and Mixed Numbers

The value of a fraction does not change if multiplying or dividing both the numerator and the denominator by the same number (other than 0). In other words, $\frac{x}{y} = \frac{a \times x}{a \times y} = \frac{x \div a}{y \div a}$, as long as a is not 0. This means that $\frac{2}{5} = \frac{4}{10}$, for example. If x and y are integers that have no common factors, then the fraction is said to be **simplified**. This means $\frac{2}{5}$ is simplified, but $\frac{4}{10}$ is not.

Often when working with fractions, the fractions need to be rewritten so that they all share a single denominator—this is called finding a **common denominator** for the fractions. Using two fractions, $\frac{a}{b}$ and $\frac{c}{d}$, the numerator and denominator of the left fraction can be multiplied by d, while the numerator and denominator of the right fraction can be multiplied by b. This provides the fractions $\frac{a \times d}{b \times d}$ and $\frac{c \times b}{d \times b}$ with the common denominator $b \times d$.

A fraction whose numerator is smaller than its denominator is called a **proper fraction**. A fraction whose numerator is bigger than its denominator is called an **improper fraction**. These numbers can be rewritten as a combination of integers and fractions, called a **mixed number**. For example:

$$\frac{6}{5} = \frac{5}{5} + \frac{1}{5} = 1 + \frac{1}{5} \text{ which can be written as: } 1\frac{1}{5}$$

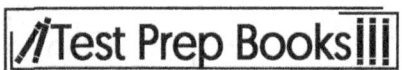

Estimating

Estimation is finding a value that is close to a solution but is not the exact answer. For example, if there are values in the thousands to be multiplied, then each value can be estimated to the nearest thousand and the calculation performed. This value provides an approximate solution that can be determined very quickly.

Recognition of Decimals

The **decimal system** is a way of writing out numbers that uses ten different numerals: 0, 1, 2, 3, 4, 5, 6, 7, 8, and 9. This is also called a "base ten" or "base 10" system. Other bases are also used. For example, computers work with a base of 2. This means they only use the numerals 0 and 1.

The **decimal place** denotes how far to the right of the decimal point a numeral is. The first digit to the right of the decimal point is in the *tenths* place. The next is the *hundredths*. The third is the *thousandths*.

So, 3.142 has a 1 in the tenths place, a 4 in the hundredths place, and a 2 in the thousandths place.

The **decimal point** is a period used to separate the *ones* place from the *tenths* place when writing out a number as a decimal.

A **decimal number** is a number written out with a decimal point instead of as a fraction, for example, 1.25 instead of $\frac{5}{4}$. Depending on the situation, it can sometimes be easier to work with fractions and sometimes easier to work with decimal numbers.

A decimal number is **terminating** if it stops at some point. It is called **repeating** if it never stops but repeats over and over. It is important to note that every rational number can be written as a terminating decimal or as a repeating decimal.

Addition with Decimals

To add decimal numbers, each number in the columns needs to be lined up by the decimal point. For each number being added, the zeros to the right of the last number need to be filled in so that each of the numbers has the same number of places to the right of the decimal. Then, the columns can be added together. Here is an example of 2.45 + 1.3 + 8.891 written in column form:

$$\begin{array}{r} 2.450 \\ 1.300 \\ + 8.891 \end{array}$$

Zeros have been added in the columns so that each number has the same number of places to the right of the decimal.

Added together, the correct answer is 12.641:

$$\begin{array}{r} 2.450 \\ 1.300 \\ + 8.891 \\ \hline 12.641 \end{array}$$

Quantitative Reasoning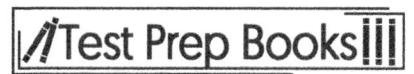

Subtraction with Decimals
Subtracting decimal numbers is the same process as adding decimals. Here is 7.89 – 4.235 written in column form:

$$\begin{array}{r} 7.890 \\ -\ 4.235 \\ \hline 3.655 \end{array}$$

A zero has been added in the column so that each number has the same number of places to the right of the decimal.

Multiplication with Decimals
The simplest way to multiply decimals is to calculate the product as if the decimals are not there, then count the number of decimal places in the original problem. Use that total to place the decimal the same number of places over in your answer, counting from right to left. For example, 0.5×1.25 can be rewritten and multiplied as 5×125, which equals 625. Then the decimal is added three places from the right for .625.

The final answer will have the same number of decimal points as the total number of decimal places in the problem. The first number has one decimal place, and the second number has two decimal places. Therefore, the final answer will contain three decimal places:

$$0.5 \times 1.25 = 0.625$$

Division with Decimals
Dividing a decimal by a whole number entails using long division first by ignoring the decimal point. Then, the decimal point is moved the number of places given in the problem.

For example, $6.8 \div 4$ can be rewritten as $68 \div 4$, which is 17. There is one non-zero integer to the right of the decimal point, so the final solution would have one decimal place to the right of the solution. In this case, the solution is 1.7.

Dividing a decimal by another decimal requires changing the divisor to a whole number by moving its decimal point. The decimal place of the dividend should be moved by the same number of places as the divisor. Then, the problem is the same as dividing a decimal by a whole number.

For example, $5.72 \div 1.1$ has a divisor with one decimal point in the denominator. The expression can be rewritten as $57.2 \div 11$ by moving each number one decimal place to the right to eliminate the decimal. The long division can be completed as $572 \div 11$ with a result of 52. Since there is one non-zero integer to the right of the decimal point in the problem, the final solution is 5.2.

In another example, $8 \div 0.16$ has a divisor with two decimal points in the denominator. The expression can be rewritten as $800 \div 16$ by moving each number two decimal places to the right to eliminate the decimal in the divisor. The long division can be completed with a result of 50.

Fraction and Percent Equivalencies
The word **percent** comes from the Latin phrase for "per one hundred." A percent is a way of writing out a fraction. It is a fraction with a denominator of 100. Thus, $65\% = \frac{65}{100}$.

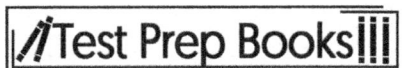

To convert a fraction to a percent, the denominator is written as 100. For example:

$$\frac{3}{5} = \frac{60}{100} = 60\%$$

In converting a percent to a fraction, the percent is written with a denominator of 100, and the result is simplified. For example:

$$30\% = \frac{30}{100} = \frac{3}{10}$$

Percent Problems

The basic percent equation is the following:

$$\frac{is}{of} = \frac{\%}{100}$$

The placement of numbers in the equation depends on what the question asks.

Example 1

Find 40% of 80.

Basically, the problem is asking, "What is 40% of 80?" The 40% is the percent, and 80 is the number to find the percent "of." The equation is:

$$\frac{x}{80} = \frac{40}{100}$$

Solving the equation by cross-multiplication, the problem becomes $100x = 80(40)$. Solving for x produces the answer: $x = 32$.

Example 2

What percent of 100 is 20?

20 fills in the "is" portion, while 100 fills in the "of." The question asks for the percent, so that will be x, the unknown. The following equation is set up:

$$\frac{20}{100} = \frac{x}{100}$$

Cross-multiplying yields the equation $100x = 20(100)$. Solving for x gives the answer: 20%.

Example 3

30% of what number is 30?

The following equation uses the clues and numbers in the problem:

$$\frac{30}{x} = \frac{30}{100}$$

14

Quantitative Reasoning

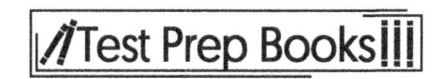

Cross-multiplying results in the equation $30(100) = 30x$. Solving for x gives the answer: $x = 100$.

Problems Involving Estimation

Sometimes when multiplying numbers, the result can be estimated by **rounding**. For example, to estimate the value of 11.2×2.01, each number can be rounded to the nearest integer. This will yield a result of 22.

Rate, Percent, and Measurement Problems

A **ratio** compares the size of one group to the size of another. For example, there may be a room with 4 tables and 24 chairs. The ratio of tables to chairs is 4: 24. Such ratios behave like fractions in that both sides of the ratio by the same number can be multiplied or divided. Thus, the ratio 4:24 is the same as the ratio 2:12 and 1:6.

One quantity is **proportional** to another quantity if the first quantity is always some multiple of the second. For instance, the distance travelled in five hours is always five times to the speed as travelled. The distance is proportional to speed in this case.

One quantity is **inversely proportional** to another quantity if the first quantity is equal to some number divided by the second quantity. The time it takes to travel one hundred miles will be given by 100 divided by the speed travelled. The time is inversely proportional to the speed.

When dealing with word problems, there is no fixed series of steps to follow, but there are some general guidelines to use. It is important that the quantity to be found is identified. Then, it can be determined how the given values can be used and manipulated to find the final answer.

Example 1

Jana wants to travel to visit Alice, who lives one hundred and fifty miles away. If she can drive at fifty miles per hour, how long will her trip take?

The quantity to find is the *time* of the trip. The time of a trip is given by the distance to travel divided by the speed to be traveled. The problem determines that the distance is one hundred and fifty miles, while the speed is fifty miles per hour. Thus, 150 divided by 50 is $150 \div 50 = 3$. Because *miles* and *miles per hour* are the units being divided, the miles cancel out. The result is 3 hours.

Example 2

Bernard wishes to paint a wall that measures twenty feet wide by eight feet high. It costs ten cents to paint one square foot. How much money will Bernard need for paint?

The final quantity to compute is the *cost* to paint the wall. This will be ten cents ($0.10) for each square foot of area needed to paint. The area to be painted is unknown, but the dimensions of the wall are given; thus, it can be calculated.

The dimensions of the wall are 20 feet wide and 8 feet high. Since the area of a rectangle is length multiplied by width, the area of the wall is $8 \times 20 = 160$ square feet. Multiplying 0.1×160 yields $16 as the cost of the paint.

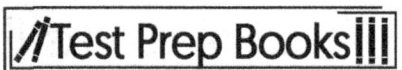

Quantitative Reasoning

The **average** or **mean** of a collection of numbers is given by adding those numbers together and then dividing by the total number of values. A **weighted average** or **weighted mean** is given by adding the numbers multiplied by their weights, then dividing by the sum of the weights:

$$\frac{w_1 x_1 + w_2 x_2 + w_3 x_3 \ldots + w_n x_n}{w_1 + w_2 + w_3 + \ldots + w_n}$$

An **ordinary average** is a weighted average where all the weights are 1.

Distribution of a Quantity into its Fractional Parts

A quantity may be broken into its fractional parts. For example, a toy box holds three types of toys for kids. $\frac{1}{3}$ of the toys are Type A and $\frac{1}{4}$ of the toys are Type B. With that information, how many Type C toys are there?

First, the sum of Type A and Type B must be determined by finding a common denominator to add the fractions. The lowest common multiple is 12, so that is what will be used. The sum is:

$$\frac{1}{3} + \frac{1}{4} = \frac{4}{12} + \frac{3}{12} = \frac{7}{12}$$

This value is subtracted from 1 to find the number of Type C toys. The value is subtracted from 1 because 1 represents a whole. The calculation is:

$$1 - \frac{7}{12} = \frac{12}{12} - \frac{7}{12} = \frac{5}{12}$$

This means that $\frac{5}{12}$ of the toys are Type C. To check the answer, add all fractions together, and the result should be 1.

Algebra

Solving for X in Proportions

Proportions are commonly used to solve word problems to find unknown values such as x that are some percent or fraction of a known number. Proportions are solved by cross-multiplying and then dividing to arrive at x. The following examples show how this is done:

1) $\frac{75\%}{90\%} = \frac{25\%}{x}$

To solve for x, the fractions must be cross multiplied:

$$75\% x = 90\% \times 25\%$$

To make things easier, let's convert the percentages to decimals:

$$0.9 \times 0.25 = 0.225 = 0.75x$$

Quantitative Reasoning

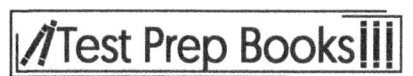

To get rid of x's coefficient, each side must be divided by that same coefficient to get the answer $x = 0.3$. The question could ask for the answer as a percentage or fraction in lowest terms, which are 30% and $\frac{3}{10}$, respectively.

2) $\frac{x}{12} = \frac{30}{96}$

Cross-multiply: $96x = 30 \times 12$
Multiply: $96x = 360$
Divide: $x = 360 \div 96$
Answer: $x = 3.75$

3) $\frac{0.5}{3} = \frac{x}{6}$

Cross-multiply: $3x = 0.5 \times 6$
Multiply: $3x = 3$
Divide: $x = 3 \div 3$
Answer: $x = 1$

You may have noticed there's a faster way to arrive at the answer. If there is an obvious operation being performed on the proportion, the same operation can be used on the other side of the proportion to solve for x. For example, in the first practice problem, 75% became 25% when divided by 3, and upon doing the same to 90%, the correct answer of 30% would have been found with much less legwork. However, these questions aren't always so intuitive, so it's a good idea to work through the steps, even if the answer seems apparent from the outset.

Translating Words into Math

To translate a word problem into an expression, look for a series of key words indicating addition, subtraction, multiplication, or division:

Addition: *add, altogether, together, plus, increased by, more than, in all, sum,* and *total*

Subtraction: *minus, less than, difference, decreased by, fewer than, remain,* and *take away*

Multiplication: *times, twice, of, double,* and *triple*

Division: *divided by, cut up, half, quotient of, split,* and *shared equally*

If a question asks to give words to a mathematical expression and says "equals," then an = sign must be included in the answer. Similarly, "less than or equal to" is expressed by the inequality symbol ≤, and "greater than or equal" to is expressed as ≥. Furthermore, "less than" is represented by <, and "greater than" is expressed by >.

Word Problems

Word problems can appear daunting, but don't let the verbiage psych you out. No matter the scenario or specifics, the key to answering them is to translate the words into a math problem. Always keep in mind what the question is asking and what operations could lead to that answer. The following word problem resembles one of the question types most frequently encountered on the exam.

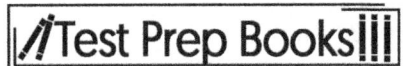

Quantitative Reasoning

Working with Money

Walter's Coffee Shop sells a variety of drinks and breakfast treats.

Price List	
Hot Coffee	$2.00
Slow-Drip Iced Coffee	$3.00
Latte	$4.00
Muffin	$2.00
Crepe	$4.00
Egg Sandwich	$5.00

Costs	
Hot Coffee	$0.25
Slow-Drip Iced Coffee	$0.75
Latte	$1.00
Muffin	$1.00
Crepe	$2.00
Egg Sandwich	$3.00

Walter's utilities, rent, and labor costs him $500 per day. Today, Walter sold 200 hot coffees, 100 slow-drip iced coffees, 50 lattes, 75 muffins, 45 crepes, and 60 egg sandwiches. What was Walter's total profit today?

To accurately answer this type of question, determine the total cost of making his drinks and treats, then determine how much revenue he earned from selling those products. After arriving at these two totals, the profit is measured by deducting the total cost from the total revenue.

Walter's costs for today:

Item	Quantity	Cost Per Unit	Total Cost
Hot Coffee	200	$0.25	$50
Slow-Drip Iced Coffee	100	$0.75	$75
Latte	50	$1.00	$50
Muffin	75	$1.00	$75
Crepe	45	$2.00	$90
Egg Sandwich	60	$3.00	$180
Utilities, rent, and labor			$500
Total Costs			$1,020

Quantitative Reasoning

Walter's revenue for today:

Item	Quantity	Revenue Per Unit	Total Revenue
Hot Coffee	200	$2.00	$400
Slow-Drip Iced Coffee	100	$3.00	$300
Latte	50	$4.00	$200
Muffin	75	$2.00	$150
Crepe	45	$4.00	$180
Egg Sandwich	60	$5.00	$300
Total Revenue			$1,530

$$\text{Walter's Profit} = \text{Revenue} - \text{Costs} = \$1,530 - \$1,020 = \$510$$

This strategy is applicable to other question types. For example, calculating salary after deductions, balancing a checkbook, and calculating a dinner bill are common word problems similar to business planning. Just remember to use the correct operations. When a balance is increased, use addition. When a balance is decreased, use subtraction. Common sense and organization are your greatest assets when answering word problems.

Unit Rate

Unit rate word problems will ask to calculate the rate or quantity of something in a different value. For example, a problem might say that a car drove a certain number of miles in a certain number of minutes and then ask how many miles per hour the car was traveling. These questions involve solving proportions. Consider the following examples:

1) Alexandra made $96 during the first 3 hours of her shift as a temporary worker at a law office. She will continue to earn money at this rate until she finishes in 5 more hours. How much does Alexandra make per hour? How much will Alexandra have made at the end of the day?

This problem can be solved in two ways. The first is to set up a proportion, as the rate of pay is constant. The second is to determine her hourly rate, multiply the 5 hours by that rate, and then add the $96.

To set up a proportion, put the money already earned over the hours already worked on one side of an equation. The other side has x over 8 hours (the total hours worked in the day). It looks like this:

$$\frac{96}{3} = \frac{x}{8}$$

Now, cross-multiply to get $768 = 3x$. To get x, divide by 3, which leaves $x = 256$. Alternatively, as x is the numerator of one of the proportions, multiplying by its denominator will reduce the solution by one step. Thus, Alexandra will make $256 at the end of the day. To calculate her hourly rate, divide the total by 8, giving $32 per hour.

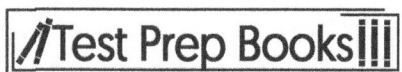

Quantitative Reasoning

Alternatively, it is possible to figure out the hourly rate by dividing $96 by 3 hours to get $32 per hour. Now her total pay can be figured by multiplying $32 per hour by 8 hours, which comes out to $256.

2) Jonathan is reading a novel. So far, he has read 215 of the 335 total pages. It takes Jonathan 25 minutes to read 10 pages, and the rate is constant. How long does it take Jonathan to read one page? How much longer will it take him to finish the novel? Express the answer in time.

To calculate how long it takes Jonathan to read one page, divide the 25 minutes by 10 pages to determine the page per minute rate. Thus, it takes 2.5 minutes to read one page.

Jonathan must read 120 more pages to complete the novel. (This is calculated by subtracting the pages already read from the total.) Now, multiply his rate per page by the number of pages. Thus,

$$120 \times 2.5 = 300$$

Expressed in time, 300 minutes is equal to 5 hours.

3) At a hotel, $\frac{4}{5}$ of the 120 rooms are booked for Saturday. On Sunday, $\frac{3}{4}$ of the rooms are booked. On which day are more of the rooms booked, and by how many more?

The first step is to calculate the number of rooms booked for each day. Do this by multiplying the fraction of the rooms booked by the total number of rooms.

Saturday: $\frac{4}{5} \times 120 = \frac{4}{5} \times \frac{120}{1} = \frac{480}{5} = 96$ rooms

Sunday: $\frac{3}{4} \times 120 = \frac{3}{4} \times \frac{120}{1} = \frac{360}{4} = 90$ rooms

Thus, more rooms were booked on Saturday by 6 rooms.

4) In a veterinary hospital, the veterinarian-to-pet ratio is 1:9. The ratio is always constant. If there are 45 pets in the hospital, how many veterinarians are currently in the veterinary hospital?

Set up a proportion to solve for the number of veterinarians:

$$\frac{1}{9} = \frac{x}{45}$$

Cross-multiplying results in $9x = 45$, which works out to 5 veterinarians.

Alternatively, as there are always 9 times as many pets as veterinarians, it is possible to divide the number of pets (45) by 9. This also arrives at the correct answer of 5 veterinarians.

5) At a general practice law firm, 30% of the lawyers work solely on tort cases. If 9 lawyers work solely on tort cases, how many lawyers work at the firm?

First, solve for the total number of lawyers working at the firm, which will be represented here with x. The problem states that 9 lawyers work solely on torts cases, and they make up 30% of the total lawyers at the firm. Thus, 30% multiplied by the total, x, will equal 9. Written as equation, this is:

$$30\% \times x = 9$$

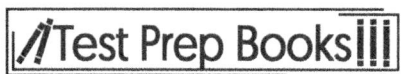

Quantitative Reasoning

It's easier to deal with the equation after converting the percentage to a decimal, leaving $0.3x = 9$. Thus, $x = \frac{9}{0.3} = 30$ lawyers working at the firm.

6) Xavier was hospitalized with pneumonia. He was originally given 35mg of antibiotics. Later, after his condition continued to worsen, Xavier's dosage was increased to 60mg. What was the percent increase of the antibiotics? Round the percentage to the nearest tenth.

An increase or decrease in percentage can be calculated by dividing the difference in amounts by the original amount and multiplying by 100. Written as an equation, the formula is:

$$\frac{\text{new quantity} - \text{old quantity}}{\text{old quantity}} \times 100$$

Here, the question states that the dosage was increased from 35mg to 60mg, so these are plugged into the formula to find the percentage increase.

$$\frac{60 - 35}{35} \times 100 = \frac{25}{35} \times 100$$

$$0.7142 \times 100 = 71.4\%$$

Order of Rational Numbers

A common question type asks to order rational numbers from least to greatest or greatest to least. The numbers will come in a variety of formats, including decimals, percentages, roots, fractions, and whole numbers. These questions test for knowledge of different types of numbers and the ability to determine their respective values.

Whether the question asks to order the numbers from greatest to least or least to greatest, the crux of the question is the same—convert the numbers into a common format. Generally, it's easiest to write the numbers as whole numbers and decimals so they can be placed on a number line. Follow these examples to understand this strategy.

1) Order the following rational numbers from greatest to least:

$$\sqrt{36}, 0.65, 78\%, \frac{3}{4}, 7, 90\%, \frac{5}{2}$$

Of the seven numbers, the whole number (7) and decimal (0.65) are already in an accessible form, so concentrate on the other five.

First, the square root of 36 equals 6. (If the test asks for the root of a non-perfect root, determine which two whole numbers the root lies between.) Next, convert the percentages to decimals. A percentage means "per hundred," so this conversion requires moving the decimal point two places to the left, leaving 0.78 and 0.9. Lastly, evaluate the fractions:

$$\frac{3}{4} = \frac{75}{100} = 0.75 \; ; \frac{5}{2} = 2\frac{1}{2} = 2.5$$

Now, the only step left is to list the numbers in the request order:

$$7, \sqrt{36}, \frac{5}{2}, 90\%, 78\%, \frac{3}{4}, 0.65$$

Quantitative Reasoning

2) Order the following rational numbers from least to greatest:

$$2.5, \sqrt{9}, -10.5, 0.853, 175\%, \sqrt{4}, \frac{4}{5}$$

$$\sqrt{9} = 3$$

$$175\% = 1.75$$

$$\sqrt{4} = 2$$

$$\frac{4}{5} = 0.8$$

From least to greatest, the answer is: -10.5, $\frac{4}{5}$, 0.853, 175%, $\sqrt{4}$, 2.5, $\sqrt{9}$,

FOIL Method

FOIL is a technique for generating polynomials through the multiplication of binomials. A polynomial is an expression of multiple variables (for example, x, y, z) in at least three terms involving only the four basic operations and exponents. FOIL is an acronym for First, Outer, Inner, and Last. "First" represents the multiplication of the terms appearing first in the binomials. "Outer" means multiplying the outermost terms. "Inner" means multiplying the terms inside. "Last" means multiplying the last terms of each binomial.

After completing FOIL and solving the operations, like terms are combined. To identify like terms, look for terms with the same variable and the same exponent. For example, look at:

$$4x^2 - x^2 + 15x + 2x^2 - 8$$

The $4x^2, -x^2$, and $2x^2$ are all like terms because they have the variable (x) and exponent (2). Thus, after combining the like terms, the polynomial has been simplified:

$$5x^2 + 15x - 8$$

The purpose of FOIL is to simplify an equation involving multiple variables and operations. Although it sounds complicated, working through some examples will provide some clarity:

1) Simplify $(x + 10)(x + 4) = (x \times x) + (x \times 4) + (10 \times x) + (10 \times 4)$
                                                          First   Outer   Inner   Last

After multiplying these binomials, it's time to solve the operations and combine like terms. Thus, the expression becomes:

$$x^2 + 4x + 10x + 40 = x^2 + 14x + 40$$

2) Simplify $2x(4x^3 - 7y^2 + 3x^2 + 4)$

Here, a monomial ($2x$) is multiplied into a polynomial:

$$(4x^3 - 7y^2 + 3x^2 + 4)$$

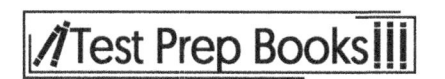

Using the distributive property, multiply the monomial against each term in the polynomial. This becomes:

$$2x(4x^3) - 2x(7y^2) + 2x(3x^2) + 2x(4).$$

Now, simplify each monomial. Start with the coefficients:

$$(2 \times 4)(x \times x^3) - (2 \times 7)(x \times y^2) + (2 \times 3)(x \times x^2) + (2 \times 4)(x)$$

When multiplying powers with the same base, add their exponents. Remember, a variable with no listed exponent has an exponent of 1, and exponents of distinct variables cannot be combined. This produces the answer:

$$8x^{1+3} - 14xy^2 + 6x^{1+2} + 8x = 8x^4 - 14xy^2 + 6x^3 + 8x$$

3) Simplify $(8x^{10}y^2z^4) \div (4x^2y^4z^7)$

First, divide the coefficients of the first two polynomials: $8 \div 4 = 2$. Second, divide exponents with the same variable, which requires subtracting the exponents. This results in:

$$2(x^{10-2}y^{2-4}z^{4-7}) = 2x^8y^{-2}z^{-3}$$

However, the most simplified answer should include only positive exponents. Thus, $y^{-2}z^{-3}$ needs to be converted into fractions, respectively $\frac{1}{y^2}$ and $\frac{1}{z^3}$. Since the $2x^8$ has a positive exponent, it is placed in the numerator, and $\frac{1}{y^2}$ and $\frac{1}{z^3}$ are combined into the denominator, leaving $\frac{2x^8}{y^2z^3}$ as the final answer.

Rational Expressions

A **rational expression** is a fraction where the numerator and denominator are both polynomials. Some examples of rational expressions include the following: $\frac{4x^3y^5}{3z^4}$, $\frac{4x^3+3x}{x^2}$, and $\frac{x^2+7x+10}{x+2}$. Since these refer to expressions and not equations, they can be simplified but not solved. Using the rules in the previous *Exponents* and *Roots* sections, some rational expressions with monomials can be simplified. Other rational expressions such as the last example, $\frac{x^2+7x+10}{x+2}$, require more steps to be simplified. First, the polynomial on top can be factored from $x^2 + 7x + 10$ into $(x + 5)(x + 2)$. Then the common factors can be canceled, and the expression can be simplified to $(x + 5)$.

The following problem is an example of using rational expressions:

Reggie wants to lay sod in his rectangular backyard. The length of the yard is given by the expression $4x + 2$, and the width is unknown. The area of the yard is $20x + 10$. Reggie needs to find the width of the yard. Knowing that the area of a rectangle is length multiplied by width, an expression can be written to find the width: $\frac{20x+10}{4x+2}$, area divided by length. Simplifying this expression by factoring out 10 on the top and 2 on the bottom leads to this expression: $\frac{10(2x+1)}{2(2x+1)}$. Cancelling out the $2x + 1$ results in $\frac{10}{2} = 5$. The width of the yard is found to be 5 by simplifying the rational expression.

Rational Equations

A **rational equation** can be as simple as an equation with a ratio of polynomials, $\frac{p(x)}{q(x)}$, set equal to a value, where $p(x)$ and $q(x)$ are both polynomials. A rational equation has an equal sign, which is different from expressions. This leads to solutions, or numbers that make the equation true.

It is possible to solve rational equations by trying to get all of the x terms out of the denominator and then isolating them on one side of the equation. For example, to solve the equation $\frac{3x+2}{2x+3} = 4$, both sides get multiplied by $(2x + 3)$. This will cancel on the left side to yield $3x + 2 = 4(2x + 3)$, then:

$$3x + 2 = 8x + 12$$

Now, subtract $8x$ from both sides, which yields:

$$-5x + 2 = 12$$

Subtracting 2 from both sides results in $-5x = 10$. Finally, both sides get divided by -5 to obtain $x = -2$.

Sometimes, when solving rational equations, it can be easier to try to simplify the rational expression by factoring the numerator and denominator first, then cancelling out common factors. For example, to solve $\frac{2x^2-8x+6}{x^2-3x+2} = 1$, the first step is to factor:

$$2x^2 - 8x + 6 = 2(x^2 - 4x + 3)$$

$$2(x - 1)(x - 3)$$

Then, factor $x^2 - 3x + 2$ into $(x - 1)(x - 2)$. This turns the original equation into:

$$\frac{2(x-1)(x-3)}{(x-1)(x-2)} = 1$$

The common factor of $(x - 1)$ can be canceled, leaving:

$$\frac{2(x-3)}{x-2} = 1$$

Now the same method used in the previous example can be followed. Multiplying both sides by $x - 1$ and performing the multiplication on the left yields $2x - 6 = x - 2$, which can be simplified to $x = 4$.

Rational Functions

A **rational function** is similar to an equation, but it includes two variables. In general, a rational function is in the form: $f(x) = \frac{p(x)}{q(x)}$, where $p(x)$ and $q(x)$ are polynomials. Refer to the *Functions* section (which follows) for a more detailed definition of functions. Rational functions are defined everywhere except where the denominator is equal to zero. When the denominator is equal to zero, this indicates either a hole in the graph or an asymptote.

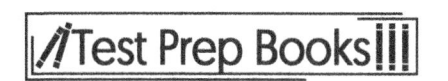

Algebraic Functions

A function is called **algebraic** if it is built up from polynomials by adding, subtracting, multiplying, dividing, and taking radicals. This means that, for example, the variable can never appear in an exponent. Thus, polynomials and rational functions are algebraic, but exponential functions are not algebraic. It turns out that logarithms and trigonometric functions are not algebraic either.

A function of the form $f(x) = a_n x^n + a_{n-1} x^{n-1} + a_{n-2} x^{n-2} + \ldots + a_1 x + a_0$ is called a **polynomial function**. The value of n is called the **degree** of the polynomial. In the case where $n = 1$, it is called a **linear function**. In the case where $n = 2$, it is called a **quadratic function**. In the case where $n = 3$, it is called a **cubic function**.

When n is even, the polynomial is called **even**, and not all real numbers will be in its range. When n is odd, the polynomial is called **odd**, and the range includes all real numbers.

The graph of a quadratic function $f(x) = ax^2 + bx + c$ will be a **parabola**. To see whether or not the parabola opens up or down, it's necessary to check the coefficient of x^2, which is the value a. If the coefficient is positive, then the parabola opens upward. If the coefficient is negative, then the parabola opens downward.

The quantity $D = b^2 - 4ac$ is called the **discriminant** of the parabola. If the discriminant is positive, then the parabola has two real zeros. If the discriminant is negative, then it has no real zeros. If the discriminant is zero, then the parabola's highest or lowest point is on the x-axis, and it has a single real zero.

The highest or lowest point of the parabola is called the **vertex**. The coordinates of the vertex are given by the point $(-\frac{b}{2a}, -\frac{D}{4a})$. The roots of a quadratic function can be found with the quadratic formula, which is:

$$x = \frac{-b \pm \sqrt{b^2 - 4ac}}{2a}$$

A **rational function** is a function $f(x) = \frac{p(x)}{q(x)}$, where p and q are both polynomials. The domain of f will be all real numbers except the (real) roots of q. At these roots, the graph of f will have a **vertical asymptote**, unless they are also roots of p. Here is an example to consider:

$$p(x) = p_n x^n + p_{n-1} x^{n-1} + p_{n-2} x^{n-2} + \ldots + p_1 x + p_0$$

$$q(x) = q_m x^m + q_{m-1} x^{m-1} + q_{m-2} x^{m-2} + \ldots + q_1 x + q_0$$

When the degree of p is less than the degree of q, there will be a **horizontal asymptote** of $y = 0$. If p and q have the same degree, there will be a horizontal asymptote of $y = \frac{p_n}{q_n}$. If the degree of p is exactly one greater than the degree of q, then f will have an oblique asymptote along the line:

$$y = \frac{p_n}{q_{n-1}} x + \frac{p_{n-1}}{q_{n-1}}$$

Plane Geometry

Locations on the plane that have no width or breadth are called **points**. These points usually will be denoted with capital letters such as P.

Any pair of points A, B on the plane will determine a unique straight line between them. This line is denoted AB. Sometimes to emphasize a line is being considered, this will be written as $\overleftrightarrow{AB}$.

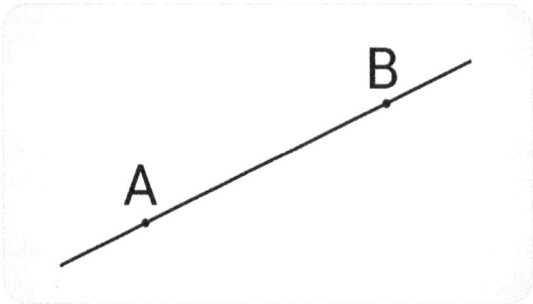

If the Cartesian coordinates for A and B are known, then the distance $d(A, B)$ along the line between them can be measured using the **Pythagorean formula**, which states that if $A = (x_1, y_1)$ and $B = (x_2, y_2)$, then the distance between them is:

$$d(A, B) = \sqrt{(x_2 - x_1)^2 + (y_2 - y_1)^2}$$

Problem Solving

The Quantitative Reasoning section of the GMAT Focus Edition is made up of 21 problem solving questions that test algebraic and arithmetic foundational knowledge. While the format and objective of each these types of questions are different, the domains of mathematics addressed in either type of question are the same and include the following:

- Arithmetic
- Elementary algebra
- Word Problems

The format of problem solving questions will likely be familiar for most test takers. These present a problem that addresses the basic mathematical skills and concepts listed above and offers five possible answer choices. Test takers must solve the problem and then select the single correct answer choice. The problem-solving questions are designed to be at a difficulty level that is on par with what is expected of an eleventh-grade student. Test takers should expect to demonstrate an understanding of elementary math concepts, reason quantitatively, and apply algebraic and arithmetic knowledge to real-world problems.

Practice Quiz

1. The value of 6 × 12 is the same as:
    a. 2 × 4 × 4 × 2
    b. 7 × 4 × 3
    c. 6 × 6 × 3
    d. 3 × 2 × 4 × 3
    e. 3 × 4 × 6 × 2

2. Dwayne has received the following scores on his math tests: 78, 92, 83, 97. What score must Dwayne get on his next math test to have an overall average of 90?
    a. 89
    b. 98
    c. 95
    d. 100
    e. 96

3. Kimberley earns $10 an hour babysitting, and after 10 p.m., she earns $12 an hour. The time she works is rounded to the nearest hour for pay purposes. On her last job, she worked from 5:30 p.m. to 11:00 p.m. In total, how much did Kimberley earn on her last job?
    a. $45
    b. $57
    c. $62
    d. $42
    e. $67

4. Arrange the following numbers from least to greatest value:
$$0.85, \frac{4}{5}, \frac{2}{3}, \frac{91}{100}$$

    a. $0.85, \frac{4}{5}, \frac{2}{3}, \frac{91}{100}$
    b. $\frac{4}{5}, 0.85, \frac{91}{100}, \frac{2}{3}$
    c. $\frac{2}{3}, \frac{4}{5}, 0.85, \frac{91}{100}$
    d. $0.85, \frac{91}{100}, \frac{4}{5}, \frac{2}{3}$
    e. $\frac{4}{5}, \frac{2}{3}, 0.85, \frac{91}{100}$

5. If $3x - 4 + 5x = 8 - 10x$, what is the value of x?
    a. 6
    b. -6
    c. 0.5
    d. 1.33
    e. 0.67

Answer Explanations

1. D: By rearranging and grouping the factors in Choice D, we can notice that $3 \times 3 \times 4 \times 2 = (3 \times 2) \times (4 \times 3) = 6 \times 12$, which is what we were looking for.

2. D: To find the average of a set of values, add the values together and then divide by the total number of values. In this case, include the unknown value of what Dwayne needs to score on his next test, in order to solve it.

$$\frac{78 + 92 + 83 + 97 + x}{5} = 90$$

Then multiply each side by 5 to simplify the equation, resulting in:

$$78 + 92 + 83 + 97 + x = 450$$
$$350 + x = 450$$
$$x = 100$$

Dwayne would need to get a perfect score of 100 in order to get an average of at least 90.

Test this answer by substituting 100 back into the original formula.

$$\frac{78 + 92 + 83 + 97 + 100}{5} = 90$$

3. C: Kimberley worked 4.5 hours at the rate of $10/h and 1 hour at the rate of $12/h. The problem states that her time is rounded to the nearest hour, so the 4.5 hours would round up to 5 hours at the rate of $10/h.

$$(5 \text{ h}) \times \left(\frac{\$10}{\text{h}}\right) + (1 \text{ h}) \times \left(\frac{\$12}{\text{h}}\right) = \$50 + \$12 = \$62$$

4. C: For each fraction, we can divide the numerator by the denominator to find a decimal value. $4/5 = 0.8$, $2/3 \approx 0.67$, and $91/100 = 0.91$. Ordering these from least to greatest gives us 0.67, 0.8, 0.85, and 0.91, which matches Choice C.

5. E: The first step in solving this equation is to collect like terms on the left side of the equation. This yields the new equation $-4 + 8x = 8 - 10x$. The next step is to move the x-terms to one side by adding $10x$ to both sides, making the equation $-4 + 18x = 8$. Then the -4 can be moved to the right side of the equation to form $18x = 12$. Dividing both sides of the equation by 18 gives a value of 0.67, or $\frac{2}{3}$.

Verbal Reasoning

Reading Comprehension

Purpose of a Passage

No matter the genre or format, all authors are writing to persuade, inform, or entertain. Often, these purposes are blended, with one dominating the rest. It's useful to learn to recognize the author's intent.

Persuasive writing is used to persuade or convince readers of something. It often contains two elements: the argument and the counterargument. The argument takes a stance on an issue, while the counterargument pokes holes in the opposition's stance. Authors rely on logic, emotion, and writer credibility to persuade readers to agree with them. If readers are opposed to the stance before reading, they are unlikely to adopt that stance. However, those who are undecided or committed to the same stance are more likely to agree with the author.

Informative writing tries to teach or inform. Workplace manuals, instructor lessons, statistical reports, and cookbooks are examples of informative texts. Informative writing is usually based on facts and void of emotion and persuasion. Informative texts generally contain statistics, charts, and graphs. Though most informative texts lack a persuasive agenda, readers still must examine the text carefully to determine whether one exists within a given passage.

Stories or narratives are designed to entertain. When people go to the movies, it's usually to escape for a few hours, not to think critically. Narrative writing is designed to delight and engage the reader. However, sometimes this type of writing can be woven into more serious materials, such as persuasive or informative writing to hook the reader before transitioning into a more scholarly discussion.

Emotional writing works to evoke the reader's feelings, such as anger, euphoria, or sadness. The connection between reader and author is an attempt to cause the reader to share the author's intended emotion or tone. Sometimes in order to make a piece more poignant, the author simply wants readers to feel the same emotions that the author has felt. Other times, the author attempts to persuade or manipulate the reader into adopting his stance. While it's okay to sympathize with the author, be aware of the individual's underlying intent.

Types of Writing Styles

Writing can be classified under four styles: narrative, expository, descriptive (sometimes called technical), and persuasive. Though these types are not mutually exclusive, one form tends to dominate the rest. By recognizing the *type* of passage you're reading, you gain insight into *how* you should read. If you're reading a narrative, you can assume the author intends to entertain, which means you may skim the text without losing meaning. A technical document might require a close read because skimming the passage might cause the reader to miss salient details.

1. **Narrative** writing, at its core, is the art of storytelling. For a narrative to exist, certain elements must be present. First, it must have characters. While many characters are human, characters could be defined as anything that thinks, acts, and talks like a human. For example, many recent movies, such as *Lord of the Rings* and *The Chronicles of Narnia*, include animals, fantastical creatures, and even trees

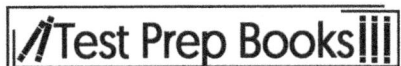

that behave like humans. Second, it must have a plot or sequence of events. Typically, those events follow a standard plot diagram, but recent trends start *in medias res* or in the middle (near the climax). In this instance, foreshadowing and flashbacks often fill in plot details. Finally, along with characters and a plot, there must also be conflict. Conflict is usually divided into two types: internal and external. Internal conflict indicates the character is in turmoil and is presented through the character's thoughts. External conflicts are visible. Types of external conflict include a person versus nature, another person, or society.

2. **Expository** writing is detached and to the point. Since expository writing is designed to instruct or inform, it usually involves directions and steps written in second person ("you" voice) and lacks any persuasive or narrative elements. Sequence words such as *first*, *second*, and *third*, or *in the first place*, *secondly*, and *lastly* are often given to add fluency and cohesion. Common examples of expository writing include instructor's lessons, cookbook recipes, and repair manuals.

3. Due to its empirical nature, **technical** writing is filled with steps, charts, graphs, data, and statistics. The goal of technical writing is to advance understanding in a field through the scientific method. Experts such as teachers, doctors, or mechanics use words unique to the profession in which they operate. These words, which often incorporate acronyms, are called **jargon**. Technical writing is a type of expository writing but is not meant to be understood by the general public. Instead, technical writers assume readers have received a formal education in a particular field of study and need no explanation as to what the jargon means. Imagine a doctor trying to understand a diagnostic reading for a car or a mechanic trying to interpret lab results. Only professionals with proper training will fully comprehend the text.

4. **Persuasive** writing is designed to change opinions and attitudes. The topic, stance, and arguments are found in the thesis, positioned near the end of the introduction. Later supporting paragraphs offer relevant quotations, paraphrases, and summaries from primary or secondary sources, which are then interpreted, analyzed, and evaluated. The goal of persuasive writers is not to stack quotes but to develop original ideas by using sources as a starting point. Good persuasive writing makes powerful arguments with valid sources and thoughtful analysis. Poor persuasive writing is riddled with bias and logical fallacies. Sometimes logical and illogical arguments are sandwiched together in the same piece. Therefore, readers should display skepticism when reading persuasive arguments.

Text Structure

Depending on what the author is attempting to accomplish, certain formats or text structures work better than others. For example, a sequence structure might work for narration but not for identifying similarities and differences between concepts. Similarly, a comparison-contrast structure is not useful for narration. It's the author's job to put the right information in the correct format.

Readers should be familiar with the five main literary structures:

1. **Sequence** structure (sometimes referred to as the order structure) is when the order of events proceed in a predictable order. In many cases, this means the text goes through the plot elements: exposition, rising action, climax, falling action, and resolution. Readers are introduced to characters, setting, and conflict in the exposition. In the rising action, there's an increase in tension and suspense. The climax is the height of tension and the point of no return. Tension decreases during the falling

action. In the resolution, any conflicts presented in the exposition are solved, and the story concludes. An informative text that is structured sequentially will often go in order from one step to the next.

2. In the **problem-solution** structure, authors identify a potential problem and suggest a solution. This form of writing is usually divided into two parts (the problem and the solution) and can be found in informational texts. For example, cell phone, cable, and satellite providers use this structure in manuals to help customers troubleshoot or identify problems with services or products.

3. When authors want to discuss similarities and differences between separate concepts, they arrange thoughts in a **comparison-contrast** paragraph structure. Venn diagrams are an effective graphic organizer for comparison-contrast structures because they feature two overlapping circles that can be used to organize similarities and differences. A comparison-contrast essay organizes one paragraph based on similarities and another based on differences. A comparison-contrast essay can also be arranged with the similarities and differences of individual traits addressed within individual paragraphs. Words such as *however*, *but*, and *nevertheless* help signal a contrast in ideas.

4. **Descriptive** writing structure is designed to appeal to your senses. Much like an artist who constructs a painting, good descriptive writing builds an image in the reader's mind by appealing to the five senses: sight, hearing, taste, touch, and smell. However, overly descriptive writing can become distracting; whereas sparse descriptions can make settings and characters seem flat. Good authors must strike a balance between the two and provide enough detail to enable the reader to really see and experience what is happening in the plot without distracting the reader with excessive details.

5. Passages that use the **cause and effect** structure are simply asking *why* by demonstrating some type of connection between ideas. Words such as *if, since, because, then, or consequently* indicate a cause-and-effect relationship. By switching the order of a complex sentence, the writer can rearrange the emphasis on different clauses. Saying, *If Sheryl is late, we'll miss the dance*, is different from saying *We'll miss the dance if Sheryl is late*. One emphasizes Sheryl's tardiness while the other emphasizes missing the dance. Paragraphs can also be arranged in a cause-and-effect format. Cause-and-effect writing discusses the impact of decisions that have been made or could be made. Researchers often apply this paragraph structure to the scientific method.

Point of View

Point of view is an important writing device to consider. In fiction writing, point of view refers to who tells the story or from whose perspective readers are observing the story. In nonfiction writing, the **point of view** refers to whether the author refers to himself/herself, their readers, or chooses not to mention either. Whether fiction or nonfiction, the author will carefully consider the impact the perspective will have on the purpose and main point of the writing.

- **First-person point of view**: The story is told from the writer's perspective. In fiction, this would mean that the main character is also the narrator. First-person point of view is easily recognized by the use of personal pronouns such as *I, me, we, us, our, my,* and *myself*.

- **Third-person point of view**: In a more formal essay, this would be an appropriate perspective because the focus should be on the subject matter, not the writer or the reader. Third-person point of view is recognized by the use of the pronouns *he, she, they,* and *it*. In fiction writing, third-person point of view has a few variations.

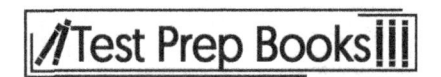

- **Third-person limited** point of view refers to a story told by a narrator who has access to the thoughts and feelings of just one character.

- In **third-person omniscient** point of view, the narrator has access to the thoughts and feelings of all the characters.

- In **third-person objective** point of view, the narrator is like a fly on the wall and can see and hear what the characters do and say but does not have access to their thoughts and feelings.

- **Second-person point of view**: This point of view isn't commonly used in fiction or nonfiction writing because it directly addresses the reader using the pronouns *you*, *your*, and *yourself*. Second-person perspective is more appropriate in direct communication, such as business letters or emails.

Point of View	Pronouns Used
First person	I, me, we, us, our, my, myself
Second person	You, your, yourself
Third person	He, she, it, they

Main Ideas and Supporting Details

Topics and main ideas are critical parts of writing. The **topic** is the subject matter of the piece. An example of a topic would be *global warming*.

The main idea is what the writer wants to say about that topic. A writer may make the point that global warming is a growing problem that must be addressed in order to save the planet. Therefore, the topic is global warming, and the main idea is that it's *a serious problem needing to be addressed*. The topic can be expressed in a word or two, but the main idea should be a complete thought.

An author will likely identify the topic immediately within the title or the first sentence of a passage. The main idea is usually presented in the introduction. In a single passage, the main idea may be identified in the first or last sentence. The main idea will most likely be easily recognized by the reader because it is what the entire paragraph or story is about. Because it is not always stated immediately in a passage, it's important to carefully read the entire passage to identify the main idea.

The main idea should not be confused with the thesis statement. A **thesis statement** is a clear statement of the writer's specific stance and can often be found in the introduction of a non-fiction piece. The thesis is a specific sentence (or two) that offers the direction and focus of the discussion.

In order to illustrate the main idea, a writer will use **supporting details**, the details that provide evidence or examples to help make a point. Supporting details often appear in the form of quotations, paraphrasing, or analysis. Authors should connect details and analysis to the main point.

For example, in the example of global warming, where the author's main idea is to show the seriousness of this growing problem and the need for change, the use of supporting details in this piece would be critical in effectively making that point. Supporting details used here might include statistics on an increase in global temperatures and studies showing the impact of global warming on the planet. The author could also include projections for future climate change in order to illustrate potential lasting effects of global warming.

Verbal Reasoning

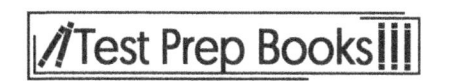

It's important to evaluate the author's supporting details to be sure that they are credible, provide evidence of the author's point, and directly support the main idea. Though shocking statistics grab readers' attention, their use could be ineffective information in the piece. Details like this are crucial to understanding the passage and evaluating how well the author presents their argument and evidence.

Also remember that when most authors write, they want to make a point or send a message. This point or message of a text is known as the theme. Authors may state themes explicitly, like in *Aesop's Fables*. More often, especially in modern literature, readers must infer the theme based on text details. Usually after carefully reading and analyzing an entire text, the reader can identify the theme. Typically, the longer the piece, the more themes you will encounter, though often one theme dominates the rest, as evidenced by the author's purposeful revisiting of it throughout the passage.

Evaluating a Passage

Determining conclusions requires being an active reader, as a reader must make a prediction and analyze facts to identify a conclusion. There are a few ways to determine a logical conclusion, but careful reading is the most important. It's helpful to read a passage a few times, noting details that seem important to the piece. A reader should also identify key words in a passage to determine the logical conclusion or determination that flows from the information presented.

Textual evidence within the details helps readers draw a conclusion about a passage. **Textual evidence** refers to information—facts and examples that support the main point. Textual evidence will likely come from outside sources and can be in the form of quoted or paraphrased material. In order to draw a conclusion from evidence, it's important to examine the credibility and validity of that evidence as well as how (and if) it relates to the main idea.

If an author presents a differing opinion or a **counterargument** in order to refute it, the reader should consider how and why the information is being presented. It is meant to strengthen the original argument and shouldn't be confused with the author's intended conclusion, but it should also be considered in the reader's final evaluation.

Sometimes, authors explicitly state the conclusion they want readers to understand. Alternatively, a conclusion may not be directly stated. In that case, readers must rely on the implications to form a logical conclusion:

> On the way to the bus stop, Michael realized his homework wasn't in his backpack. He ran back to the house to get it and made it back to the bus just in time.

In this example, though it's never explicitly stated, it can be inferred that Michael is a student on his way to school in the morning. When forming a conclusion from implied information, it's important to read the text carefully to find several pieces of evidence to support the conclusion.

Summarizing is an effective way to draw a conclusion from a passage. A summary is a shortened version of the original text, written by the reader in their own words. Focusing on the main points of the original text and including only the relevant details can help readers reach a conclusion. It's important to retain the original meaning of the passage.

Like summarizing, **paraphrasing** can also help a reader fully understand different parts of a text. Paraphrasing calls for the reader to take a small part of the passage and list or describe its main points.

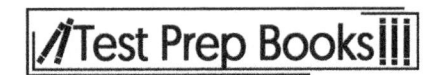

Paraphrasing is more than rewording the original passage, though. It should be written in the reader's own words, while still retaining the meaning of the original source. This will indicate an understanding of the original source, yet still help the reader expand on their interpretation.

Readers should pay attention to the **sequence**, or the order in which details are laid out in the text, as this can be important to understanding its meaning as a whole. Writers will often use transitional words to help the reader understand the order of events and to stay on track. Words like *next, then, after*, and *finally* show that the order of events is important to the author. In some cases, the author omits these transitional words, and the sequence is implied. Authors may even purposely present the information out of order to make an impact or have an effect on the reader. An example might be when a narrative writer uses **flashback** to reveal information.

Responding to a Passage and Making Inferences

There are a few ways for readers to engage actively with the text, such as making inferences and predictions. An **inference** refers to a point that is implied (as opposed to directly stated) by the evidence presented:

> Bradley packed up all of the items from his desk in a box and said goodbye to his coworkers for the last time.

From this sentence, though it is not directly stated, readers can infer that Bradley is leaving his job. It's necessary to use inference in order to draw conclusions about the meaning of a passage. Authors make implications through character dialogue, thoughts, effects on others, actions, and looks. Like in life, readers must assemble all the clues to form a complete picture.

When making an inference about a passage, it's important to rely only on the information that is provided in the text itself. This helps readers ensure that their conclusions are valid.

Readers will also find themselves making predictions when reading a passage or paragraph. **Predictions** are guesses about what's going to happen next. Readers can use prior knowledge to help make accurate predictions. Prior knowledge is best utilized when readers make links between the current text, previously read texts, and life experiences. Some texts use suspense and foreshadowing to captivate readers:

A cat darted across the street just as the car came careening around the curve.

One unfortunate prediction might be that the car will hit the cat. Of course, predictions aren't always accurate, so it's important to read carefully to the end of the text to determine the accuracy of predictions.

Critical Reasoning

It's important to read any piece of writing critically. In the Critical Reasoning sections of the GMAT Focus Edition, individuals will be tested on their ability to make arguments, evaluate arguments, and create or correct a plan of action.

Verbal Reasoning

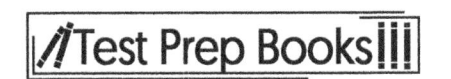

To evaluate an argument, the goal is to discover the point and purpose of what the author is writing about through analysis. It's also crucial to establish the point or stance the author has taken on the topic of the piece. After determining the author's perspective, readers can then more effectively develop their own viewpoints on the subject of the piece.

In most of the Critical Reasoning section, test takers will face questions that ask them to read a short text, evaluate the argument, and then select which answer choice either strengthens or weakens the argument, tells why the argument is flawed, or strongly supports or damages the argument. Test takers will not need specialized knowledge of the content to answer these questions.

Here is an example of a critical reasoning question:

The United States' economy continues to grow. Over the last decade, the country's Gross Domestic Product—the monetary value of all finished goods and services produced within a country's borders—has increased by between 2 and 4 percent. The United States' economy is guaranteed to grow between 2 and 4 percent next year.

> The flawed reasoning in which of the following arguments most mirrors the flawed reasoning presented in the argument above?
>
> a. Ted is obsessed with apple pie. He's consumed one whole pie every day for the last decade. Ted will probably eat a whole apple pie tomorrow.
> b. Last year Alexandra finished as the top salesperson at her company. She will undoubtedly be the top salesperson next year.
> c. George always brushes his teeth right before getting into bed. His bedtime routine has remained the same for two decades. It's more probable than not that George brushes his teeth right before getting into bed tomorrow night.
> d. Germany's economy is the strongest it's been since the end of World War II. Over the last decade, the country's Gross Domestic Product—the monetary value of all finished goods and services produced within a country's borders—has increased by between 2 and 4 percent. Germany's economic growth is a result of inclusive democratic processes.
> e. Tito is the top ranked surfer in the world. Las Vegas bookmakers listed him as a clear favorite to win the upcoming invitational tournament. Tito is more likely to win the invitational than any other surfer.

The question presents a situation and ask test takers to select an answer choice that mirrors the flawed reasoning in the argument. When solving these types of questions, test takers should read through every answer choice to find the one that aligns best with the question.

In this case, Choice *B* is the correct answer choice. Like the argument, it takes past events and speculates that conditions will not change. Just as any number of factors could alter the United States' economic growth, it is similarly unreasonable to say that Alexandra will be the top salesperson based on one year's data. This answer choice also uses extremely strong language in its speculation (*guaranteed* and *undoubtedly*).

Choice *A* is similar to the argument in that it makes a prediction based on past events; however, Choice *A*'s argument is much more reasonable than the argument. If Ted has eaten an apple pie every day for the last decade, then it's reasonable to assume that he will do so again tomorrow.

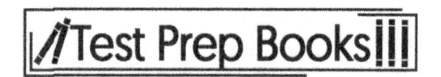

Choice C is similar to the argument, but its conclusion is much more reasonable. If George has brushed his teeth right before bed for twenty years, then it is not unreasonable to speculate that he will do the same tonight. This is not the same as predicting that past economic conditions will continue into the future. George has much more control over brushing his teeth than the United States has over its economy.

Choice D mirrors the language as the argument, but it draws a very different conclusion. In contrast to the argument, Choice D's conclusion gives a reason why Germany's economy is on the rise. It does not make a guarantee of future growth. This is not the same as the argument.

Choice E does not rely on flawed reasoning, so it must be incorrect. If Tito is the top ranked surfer in the world and listed as a clear favorite, then it's true that he's the most likely to win the tournament.

Therefore, Choice B is the correct answer, and it's confirmed by the fact that all of the other answer choices are incorrect.

Critical Thinking Skills

Critical readers examine the facts used to support an author's argument. They check the facts against other sources to be sure those facts are correct. They also check the validity of the sources used to be sure those sources are credible, academic, and/or peer reviewed. Consider that when an author uses another person's opinion to support their argument, even if it is an expert's opinion, it is still only an opinion and should not be taken as fact. A strong argument uses valid, measurable facts to support ideas. Even then, the reader may disagree with the argument as it may be rooted in their personal beliefs.

An authoritative argument may use the facts to sway the reader. Because of this, a writer may choose to only use the information and expert opinion that supports their viewpoint.

If the argument is that wind energy is the best solution, the author will use facts that support this idea. That same author may leave out relevant facts on solar energy. The way the author uses facts can influence the reader, so it's important to consider the facts being used, how those facts are being presented, and what information might be left out.

Critical readers should also look for errors in the argument such as logical fallacies and bias. A **logical fallacy** is a flaw in the logic used to make the argument. Logical fallacies include slippery slope, straw man, and begging the question. Authors can also reflect **bias** if they ignore an opposing viewpoint or present their side in an unbalanced way. A strong argument considers the opposition and finds a way to refute it. Critical readers should look for an unfair or one-sided presentation of the argument and be skeptical, as a bias may be present. Even if this bias is unintentional, if it exists in the writing, the reader should be wary of the validity of the argument.

Readers should also look for the use of **stereotypes**. These are the overly simplified beliefs about a person, place, thing, etc. that is indiscriminately applied to a larger group. These can be positive but are usually negative in nature. When a reader comes across the use of stereotypes, they should take that into consideration as they analyze the author's argument. These should generally be avoided. Stereotypes reveal a flaw in the writer's thinking and may suggest a lack of knowledge or understanding about the subject.

Verbal Reasoning

Constructing Arguments Through Evidence

Using only one form of supporting evidence is not nearly as effective as using a variety to support a claim. Presenting only a list of statistics can be boring to the reader, but providing a true story that's both interesting and humanizing helps. In addition, one example isn't always enough to prove the writer's larger point, so combining it with other examples in the writing is extremely effective. Thus, when reading a passage, readers should not just look for a single form of supporting evidence.

For example, although most people can't argue with the statement, "Seat belts save lives," its impact on the reader is much greater when supported by additional content. The writer can support this idea by:

- Providing statistics on the rate of highway fatalities alongside statistics of estimated seat belt usage.

- Explaining the science behind car accidents and what happens to a passenger who doesn't use a seat belt.

- Offering anecdotal evidence or true stories from reliable sources on how seat belts prevent fatal injuries in car crashes.

Another key aspect of supporting evidence is a **reliable source**. Does the writer include the source of the information? If so, is the source well-known and trustworthy? Is there a potential for bias? For example, a seat belt study done by a seat belt manufacturer may have its own agenda to promote.

Tone

Tone refers to the writer's attitude toward the subject matter. Tone is usually explained in terms of a work of fiction. For example, the tone conveys how the writer feels about their characters and the situations in which they're involved.

A lot of nonfiction writing has a neutral tone, which is an important tone for the writer to take. A neutral tone demonstrates that the writer is presenting a topic impartially and letting the information speak for itself. On the other hand, nonfiction writing can be just as effective and appropriate if the tone isn't neutral. For instance, take this example involving seat belts:

> Seat belts save more lives than any other automobile safety feature. Many studies show that airbags save lives as well; however, not all cars have airbags. For instance, some older cars don't. Furthermore, air bags aren't entirely reliable. For example, studies show that in 15% of accidents airbags don't deploy as designed, but, on the other hand, seat belt malfunctions are extremely rare. The number of highway fatalities has plummeted since laws requiring seat belt usage were enacted.

In this passage, the writer mostly chooses to retain a neutral tone when presenting information. If the writer would instead include their own personal experience of losing a friend or family member in a car accident, the tone would change dramatically. The tone would no longer be neutral and would show that the writer has a personal stake in the content, allowing them to interpret the information in a different way. When analyzing tone, consider what the writer is trying to achieve in the text and how they *create* the tone using style.

Practice Quiz

Reading Comprehension

Questions 1–3 are based on the following passage:

> The town of Alexandria, Virginia was founded in 1749. Between the years 1810 and 1861, this thriving seaport was the ideal location for slave owners such as Joseph Bruin, Henry Hill, Isaac Franklin, and John Armfield to build several slave trade office structures, including slave holding areas. After 1830, when the manufacturing-based economy slowed down in Virginia, slaves were traded to plantations in the Deep South, in Alabama, Mississippi, and Louisiana. Joseph Bruin, one of the most notorious of the slave traders operating in Alexandria, alone purchased hundreds of slaves from 1844 to 1861. Harriet Beecher Stowe claimed that the horrible slave traders mentioned in her novel, *Uncle Tom's Cabin*, are reminiscent of the coldhearted Joseph Bruin. The Franklin and Armfield Office was known as one of the largest slave trading companies in the country up to the end of the Civil War period. Slaves, waiting to be traded, were held in a two-story slave pen built behind the Franklin and Armfield Office structure on Duke Street in Alexandria. Yet, many people fought to thwart these traders and did everything they could to rescue and free slaves. Two Christian African American slave sisters, with the help of northern abolitionists who bought their freedom, escaped Bruin's plan to sell them into southern prostitution. In 1861, Joseph Bruin was captured and imprisoned and his property confiscated. The Bruin Slave Jail became the Fairfax County courthouse until 1865. The original Franklin and Armfield Office building still stands in Virginia and is registered in the National Register of Historic Places. The Bruin Slave Jail is still standing on Duke Street in Alexandria but is not open to the public. The history of the slave trading enterprise is preserved and presented to the public by the Northern Virginia Urban League.

1. Based on the above passage, which of the following statements about the town of Alexandria are true?
    a. Alexandria was a seaport town that could not prosper, even with the advent of a slave trade business, because the manufacturing industry was not enough to stabilize the economy.
    b. Slave traders such as Joseph Bruin, Henry Hill, Isaac Franklin, and John Armfield rented both slave trade office buildings and slave holding buildings from landlords of Old Town, Alexandria.
    c. For over fifteen years, Joseph Bruin, a notorious slave trader, probably the one characterized in *Uncle Tom's Cabin*, bought hundreds of slaves with the intention of sending the purchased slaves to southern states such as Alabama, Mississippi, and Louisiana.
    d. The Bruin Slave Jail is open to the public; the building is located in downtown Alexandria, and still stands in Virginia. The jail is registered in the National Register of Historic Places. The history of the slave trading enterprise is preserved and presented to the public by the Northern Virginia Urban League.
    e. Isaac Franklin and John Armfield's slave-trade office structures, including slave holding areas in downtown Alexandria, did not remain open for their slave trade business until the end of the Civil War.

Verbal Reasoning

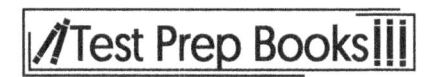

2. The passage about the Alexandria slave trade business suggests that which of the following statements can be regarded as true?
    a. The lucrative seaport town of Alexandria was supported by the successful slave trade businesses of men like Joseph Bruin, Henry Hill, Isaac Franklin, and John Armfield, who bought slaves and sold them to the plantations in the Deep South.
    b. Joseph Bruin, a highly respected Alexandrian businessman, ran a slave trade business in downtown Alexandria until the business closed its doors at the end of the Civil War.
    c. The Franklin and Armfield Office was built by Isaac Franklin and John Armfield. Slaves, waiting to be traded, were held in a four-story slave pen built behind the Franklin and Armfield Office structure on Duke Street in Alexandria.
    d. When the Confederate Army positioned its command in Alexandria and closed slave traders' businesses, the Franklin and Armfield slave pen became the Fairfax County courthouse and was used to hold Union soldiers.
    e. Literature about the slave trading enterprise, like *Uncle Tom's Cabin*, is being preserved and presented to the public by the Northern Virginia Urban League.

3. Which of the following statements best illustrates the author's intended main point or thesis?
    a. Two Christian African American slave sisters, with the help of northern abolitionists who bought their freedom, escaped Bruin's plan to sell them into southern prostitution.
    b. The town of Alexandria, a thriving seaport founded in 1749, was the location for several lucrative slave trading companies from 1810 to 1861.
    c. After the start of the Civil War, Joseph Bruin was captured and his jail was no longer used for his slave trade business.
    d. The Bruin Slave Jail is still standing on Duke Street in Alexandria but is not open to the public.
    e. In 1861, the Bruin Slave Jail in Alexandria became the Fairfax County courthouse.

Critical Reasoning

4. The "complete protein" is a source of protein that contains all nine of the essential amino acids necessary for our dietary needs. The complete protein is found in meat. Therefore, everyone should eat meat to fulfill their protein needs.
Which of the following, if true, would most weaken the above argument?
    a. Grass-fed beef is the most ethical way to buy meat to fulfill your protein needs.
    b. Legumes such as beans, seeds, or lentils mixed with grains such as pasta, rice, or corn creates a complete protein.
    c. Amino acids are necessary for humans to ingest; the body cannot make its own amino acids.
    d. Fruits and vegetables contain essential fiber, vitamins, and minerals that help our bodies fight disease.
    e. Everyone should eat more fats because they are good for your skin and hair, and help energize your body.

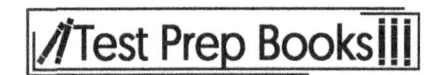

5. John looks like a professional bodybuilder. He weighs 210 pounds and stands six feet tall, which is the size of an NFL linebacker. John looks huge when he enters the room. Years of gym time have clearly paid off in spades.

Which of the following, if true, weakens the argument?
    a. John prefers to work out in the morning.
    b. The average professional bodybuilder is considerably heavier and taller than the average NFL linebacker.
    c. John weighed considerably less before he started working out.
    d. John's father, brothers, and male cousins all look like professional bodybuilders, and none of them have ever worked out.
    e. John works out five times every week.

Answer Explanations

Reading Comprehension

1. C: Choice *A* is incorrect because the seaport is noted as "thriving." Choice *B* is incorrect because the slave traders actually built both office structures and slave holding buildings in downtown Alexandria; there is no mention of renting, or of landlords. Choice *C* is correct because Joseph Bruin bought hundreds of slaves during the years 1844 to 1861. Choice *D* is incorrect because the Bruin Slave Jail is stated as NOT open to the public. Choice *E* is incorrect because the passage notes that the offices and slave holding units were open until the end of the Civil War.

2. A: Choices *B*, *C*, *D*, and *E* can all be regarded as false based on the information provided in the passage. Choice *A* contains information provided in the passage; therefore, the statement is true. Choice *B* is false because the passage states that Joseph Bruin was imprisoned in 1861; it does not say that his business lasted until the end of the Civil War. Choice *C* is false because the slave pen was not four stories high; the passage specifically noted that the slave pen was two stories high. Choice *D* is false because the passage does not refer to Union or Confederate soldiers, and the Bruin Slave Jail was what became the Fairfax County courthouse. Choice *E* is false because there is no information in the passage that indicates that literature, like *Uncle Tom's Cabin*, was preserved by the Northern Virginia Urban League.

3. C: The purpose of the passage is to shed light on the history of Joseph Bruin's Slave Jail and what became of it. Choice *A* is incorrect because while the two sisters are mentioned in the story to provide details, they are not the main purpose of the story. Choice *B* is incorrect because while the beginning of the story contains the information about the town and its slave business, this answer option leaves out the fact that the passage is focused on one slave jail in particular and omits anything about the conclusion of the passage, which is actually key in the main focus of the passage—how Joseph Bruin's Slave Jail came about and what became of it. Choice *D* is incorrect because the point of the passage is not about where the historical Bruin Slave Jail currently stands but the history behind it.

Critical Reasoning

4. B: Choice *A* is incorrect because it offers continued advice for those who agree with the statement.

Choice *B* is the correct answer choice. The speaker's argument says that everyone should eat meat because the only way to fulfill protein needs is from the complete protein in meat. However, if the statement were introduced into the argument that complete protein could be created in an alternative way than simply eating meat, it would weaken the speaker's original argument. Choice *B* is the best choice.

Choice *C* is incorrect. Facts about amino acids would not weaken the presented argument. This information acts as background context for the presented argument.

Choice *D* is misleading. The answer choice states that fruits and vegetables contain essential nutrients that help our bodies fight disease. This doesn't strengthen or weaken the original argument; it's a distractor.

Choice *E* is also a distractor, like Choice *D*. It doesn't strengthen or weaken the original argument, it just provides different information about nutrients.

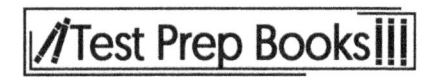

Therefore, Choice *B* is the correct answer.

5. D: Choice *A* is irrelevant. The argument makes no mention as to when John works out. Would it weaken the conclusion—which is that years of gym time have clearly paid off—if he works out in the morning instead of the afternoon? No, of course not. Eliminate this choice.

Choice *B* preys on those who incorrectly identify the conclusion. Test takers who identify the first sentence as the conclusion will find this answer very appealing. If John is the size of an NFL linebacker, but linebackers are much smaller than professional bodybuilders, then John doesn't look like a professional linebacker. However, Choice *B* is irrelevant as to whether years of working out have paid off. Eliminate this choice.

Choice *C* actually strengthens the argument. If John weighed considerably less before working out and now he looks like a professional bodybuilder, then years of working out have definitely paid off. Eliminate this choice.

Choice *D* looks very appealing. If John's family members are all similar in size without weightlifting, then it's possible that it doesn't matter that John regularly spends time in the gym. Even without lifting, John would likely be the same size as his male family members. Therefore, years of working out would not be the reason why he looks like a professional bodybuilder. Don't be concerned that Choice *D* is unlikely in reality. If a question says something's true, then treat it as true. Keep this choice for now.

Choice *E* reinforces the argument's conclusion. The argument already states that John has gone to the gym for years. Whether he goes three, five, or seven times per week does not weaken the argument. Eliminate this choice.

Therefore, Choice *D* is the correct answer.

Data Insights

Data Sufficiency

Test takers should expect to see data sufficiency problems in the Data Insights section of the GMAT Focus Edition. For these questions, rather than needing to apply quantitative reasoning methods to explicitly solve the problem, test takers must review the provided information in relation to the posed question and determine if the provided information is sufficient to answer the question.

The data sufficiency questions provide a problem and then two statements labeled 1 and 2. Following this information, five answer choices, which will be identical for all data sufficiency questions, are presented.

Test takers must select the single valid choice for each data sufficiency question from the following five options:

   A. Statement (1) ALONE is sufficient, but statement (2) alone is not sufficient to answer the question asked.
   B. Statement (2) ALONE is sufficient, but statement (1) alone is not sufficient to answer the question asked.
   C. BOTH statements (1) and (2) TOGETHER are sufficient to answer the question asked, but NEITHER statement ALONE is sufficient to answer the question asked.
   D. EACH statement ALONE is sufficient to answer the question asked.
   E. Statements (1) and (2) TOGETHER are NOT sufficient to answer the question asked, and additional data specific to the problem are needed.

Essentially, test takers must determine if just statement 1 *or* statement 2 alone provide enough information to solve the problem, if both statements are needed to arrive at the answer, if either has enough information (such that statement 1 could be used alone to solve the problem or statement 2 alone, but both aren't necessary), or if the problem cannot be solved even with all of the information put together from both.

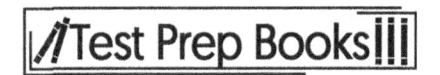

The flowchart that follows visually depicts the thinking process required by data sufficiency questions:

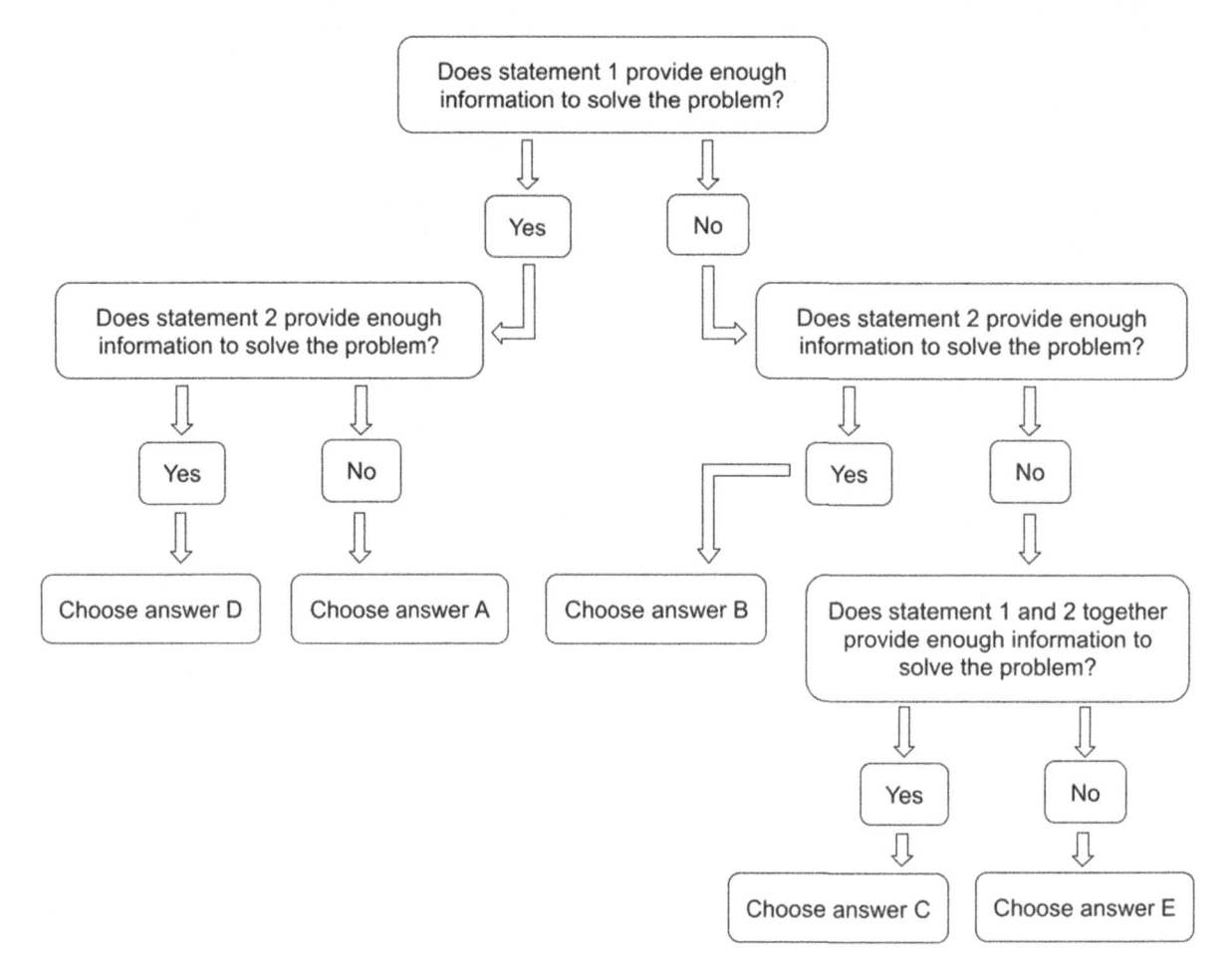

```
                    Does statement 1 provide enough
                    information to solve the problem?
                              │         │
                             Yes        No
                              ↓         ↓
  Does statement 2 provide enough    Does statement 2 provide enough
  information to solve the problem?  information to solve the problem?
           │         │                        │         │
          Yes        No                      Yes        No
           ↓         ↓                        ↓         ↓
    Choose      Choose              Choose       Does statement 1 and 2 together
    answer D    answer A            answer B     provide enough information to
                                                 solve the problem?
                                                        │         │
                                                       Yes        No
                                                        ↓         ↓
                                                   Choose      Choose
                                                   answer C    answer E
```

The good news is that test takers should not need to read through each of the five answer choices for every data sufficiency question because they will always be exactly the same and in the same order. By memorizing the answer options, test takers can save some time and bank it to use on actually working through the problems themselves. It is usually time efficient to consider statement 1 in isolation first, then statement 2, and determine if either alone provides information sufficient to solve the problem, or if both are needed. It is important for test takers to take the time to evaluate if either statement can be used in isolation to solve the problem and not just select one of the two because Choice *D* states that statement 1 alone *and* statement 2 alone contain enough information to solve the problem.

Graphics Interpretation

Identifying Information from a Graphic

Texts may have graphic representations to help illustrate and visually support assertions made. For example, graphics can be used to express samples or segments of a population or demonstrate growth or decay. Four of the most popular graphic formats include tables, bar graphs, line graphs, and pie charts.

Data Insights

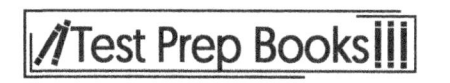

Line graphs rely on a horizontal X-axis and a vertical Y-axis to establish baseline values. A point is plotted for each data value where the x-value and y-value of the data point intersect the axes, and those points are connected with lines. Compared to bar graphs or pie charts, line graphs are more useful for looking at the past and present and predicting future outcomes. For instance, a potential investor would look for stocks that demonstrated steady growth over many decades when examining the stock market. Note that severe spikes up and down indicate instability, while line graphs that display a slow but steady increase may indicate good returns.

Bar Graphs
Here's an example of a bar graph:

Tablet Model Price Comparison

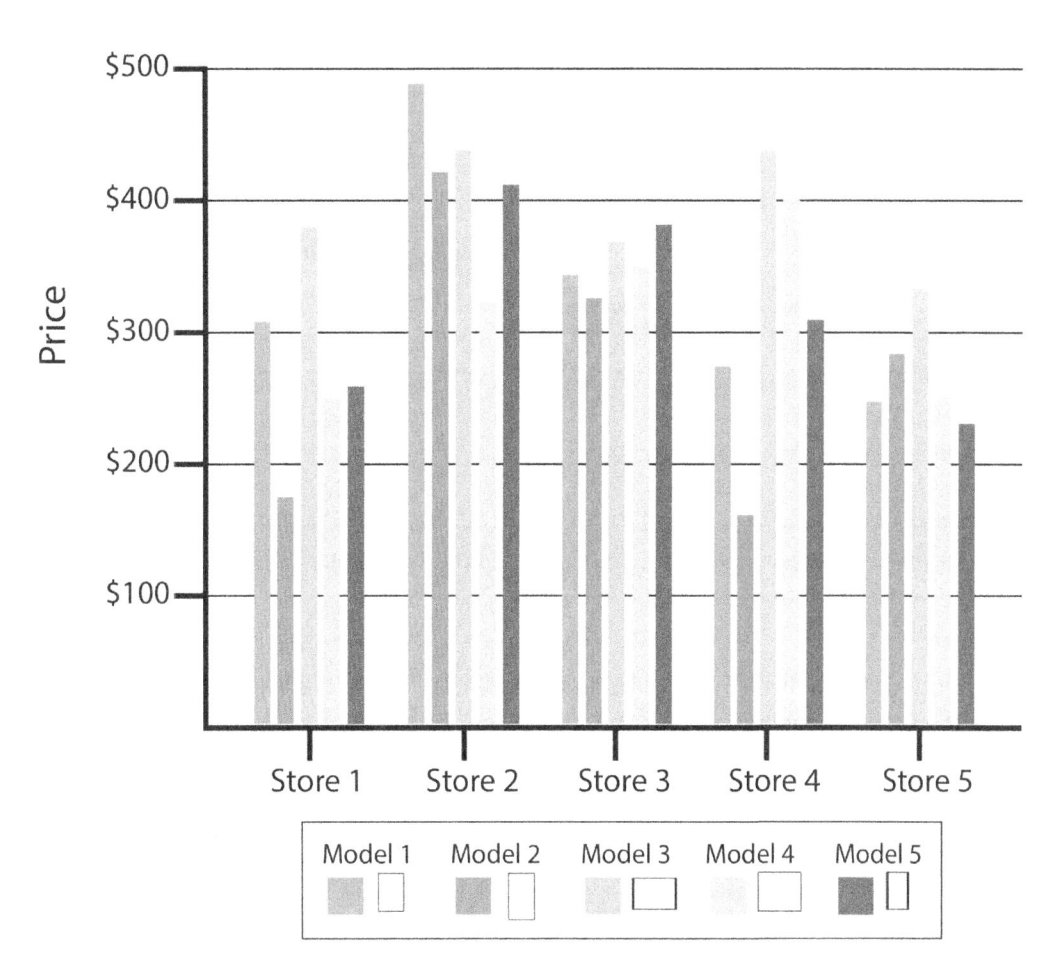

Bar graphs are usually displayed on a vertical Y-axis. The bars themselves can be two- or three-dimensional, depending on the designer's tastes. Unlike a line graph, which shows the fluctuation of only one variable, the X-axis on a bar graph is excellent for making comparisons because it shows differences between several variables. For instance, if an electronics store wanted to visually represent the number tablet sales for the year, a bar graph could have a bar for each type of tablet offered. To provide additional information, the store could show quarterly sales by constructing a bar for each type of tablet for each quarter in the fiscal year. The height of the bar would indicate the number of sales.

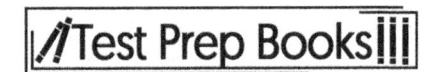

The tablet types would be displayed along the x-axis with groups of four bars per tablet—one for each quarter.

Line Graphs

Like a scatter plot, a **line graph** compares variables that change continuously, typically over time. Paired data values (ordered pair) are plotted on a coordinate grid with the x- and y-axis representing the variables. A line is drawn from each point to the next, going from left to right. The line graph below displays cell phone use for given years (two variables) for men, women, and both sexes (three data sets).

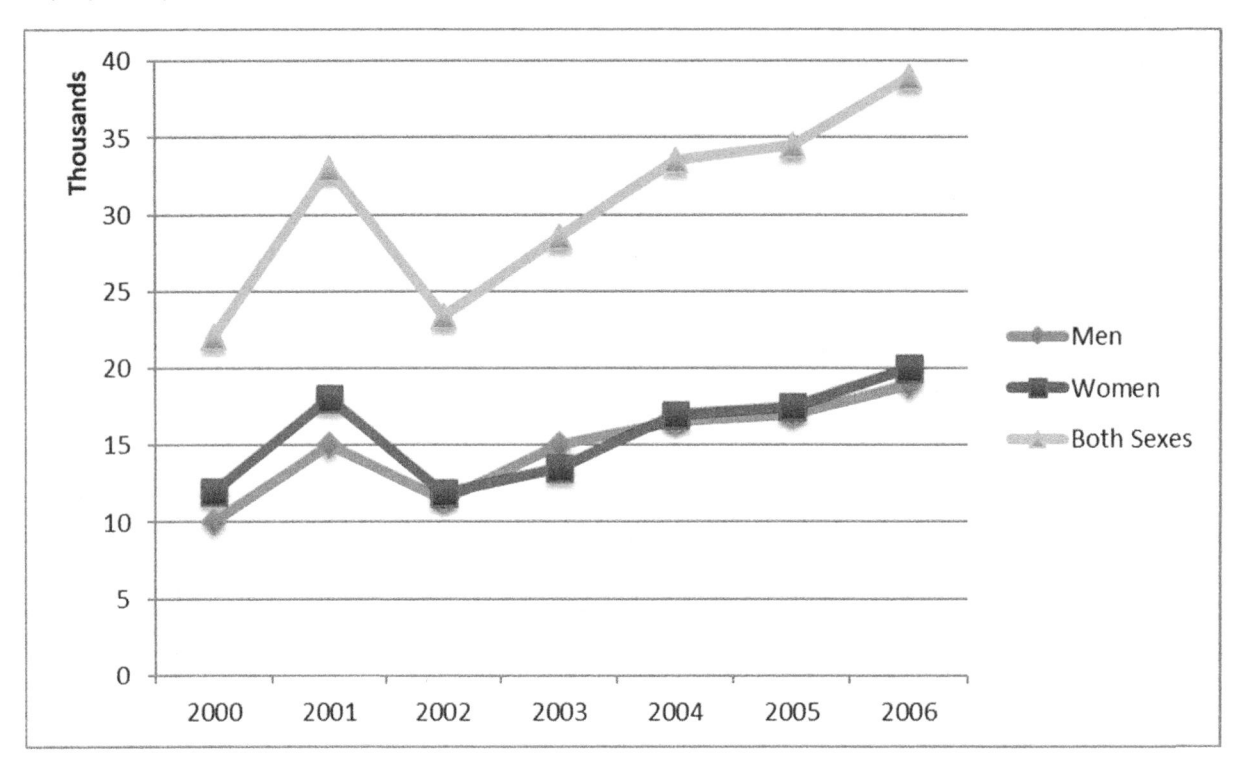

X/Y Graphs

When a linear equation is written in standard form, $Ax + By = C$, it is easy to identify the x- and y-intercepts for the graph of the line. Just as the y-intercept is the point at which the line intercepts the y-axis, the x-intercept is the point at which the line intercepts the x-axis. At the y-intercept, $x = 0$, and at the x-intercept, $y = 0$. Given an equation in standard form, substitute $x = 0$ to find the y-intercept, and substitute $y = 0$ to find the x-intercept. For example, to graph $3x + 2y = 6$, substituting 0 for y results in $3x + 2(0) = 6$. Solving for x yields $x = 2$; therefore, an ordered pair for the line is $(2, 0)$. Substituting

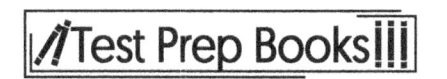

0 for x results in $3(0) + 2y = 6$. Solving for y yields $y = 3$; therefore, an ordered pair for the line is $(0, 3)$. Plot the two ordered pairs (the x- and y-intercepts), and construct a straight line through them.

T - chart

x	y
0	3
2	0

Intercepts

x - intercept : (2,0)

y - intercept : (0,3)

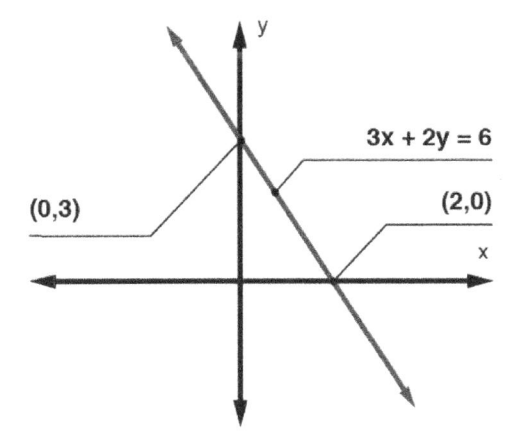

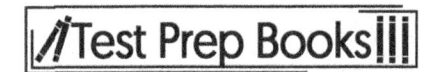

Recognizing Relationships in the Information

Pie Charts

A pie chart can depict multiple layers of information, especially when compared against other similarly constructed charts.

For example, the following pie charts can demonstrate sizable amounts of data over the course of time.

Populations of Countries of the European Union in 1998 and 2007 by percentage

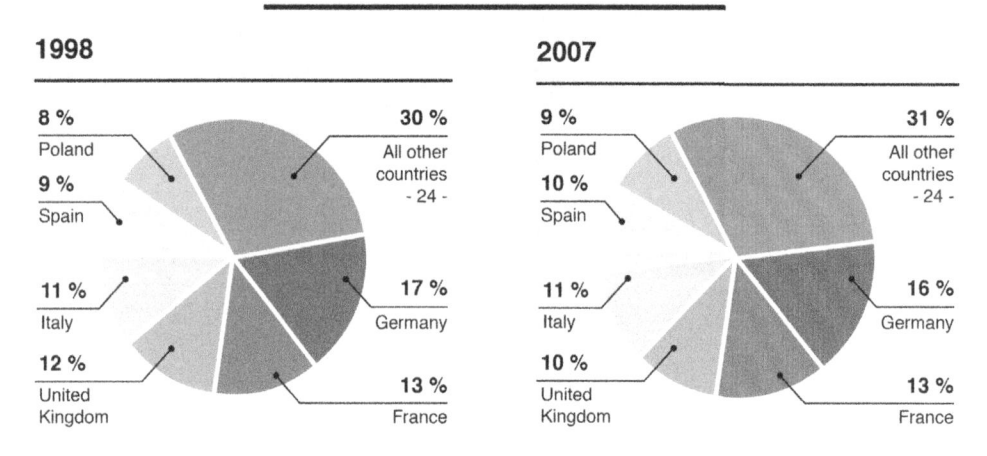

1998
- 8% Poland
- 9% Spain
- 11% Italy
- 12% United Kingdom
- 13% France
- 17% Germany
- 30% All other countries - 24 -

2007
- 9% Poland
- 10% Spain
- 11% Italy
- 10% United Kingdom
- 13% France
- 16% Germany
- 31% All other countries - 24 -

When putting such charts next to each other, it is easy to look at similarities and differences over the course of time, or among elements of the charts. The importance of such tools is observed in the ease of comparing multiple strings of data at once rather than being limited to simply one or two variables.

Relationships between similar measures can provide insight into correlations from year to year or product to product.

For example, the following graph can show a close positive correlation between the time students spend studying and their grades. This means that as the time spent studying increases, the students' grades also increase.

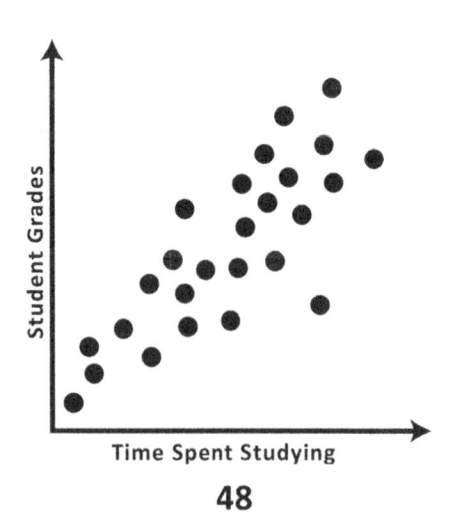

Student Grades vs. Time Spent Studying

Data Insights

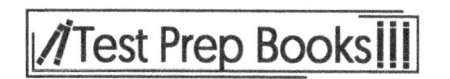

There can also be a negative correlation between variables. For example, the following graph shows a negative correlation between the number of missed classes and a student's exam score. It can be observed that the more classes a student misses, the lower the student's scores register.

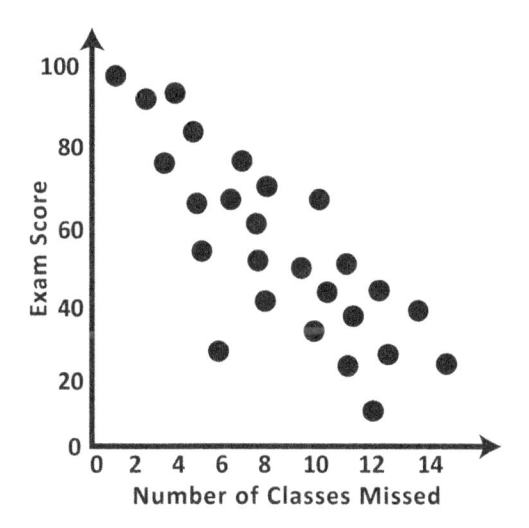

It can be a little less obvious when trying to identify relationships in information given via emails, or opinion-based writings. Generally, most business-based communications are dealing with a common topic that would need to be addressed at a meeting, such as a product, a marketing strategy, or production cost versus profit estimate. It can be difficult to decipher what the motivating factor might be for an employee's stance, but often the employee's role in the company can disclose what area he or she is going to regard as most important.

For example, a letter from the marketing expert in a company might discuss the best way to get a product out to the public and begin to register sales, while a financial expert for the same company may want to discuss the same product but discontinue its production due to the lack of profit potential compared to some unforeseen production costs. While both have the same topic in mind for discussion at a meeting, their stances on the future of the product differ. It is important to analyze any information given by each person's writing to understand their motivating factors and, thus, their position on a topic.

Multi-Source Reasoning

Multi-source reasoning questions on the GMAT Focus Edition measure test takers' abilities to use data from multiple sources and apply it real-world situations. The questions may involve recognizing data discrepancies, drawing inferences from the information, or determining relevant data.

When approaching the Data Sufficiency section of the GMAT Focus Edition, it is important to use all the information provided. Such information can be given from multiple sources, including tables, charts, graphs, and small excerpts from emails or articles. When viewing information, separate out key pieces, such as specific numbers that might determine a trend within a table or in a report of performance or sales. All sources should be labeled, thus making it easier to ascertain the relevance or importance of the data. Take an overall view of a table for the range of numbers and the headings of each column and row. On graphs or charts, the *x* and *y* axes (or horizontal and vertical lines) should be labeled with the value they are measuring, along with the base units for the measurements.

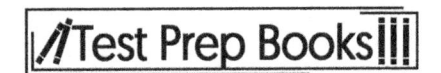

For example, the following position versus time graph is measured in meters per second, and the slope of the line can be determined to find the velocity.

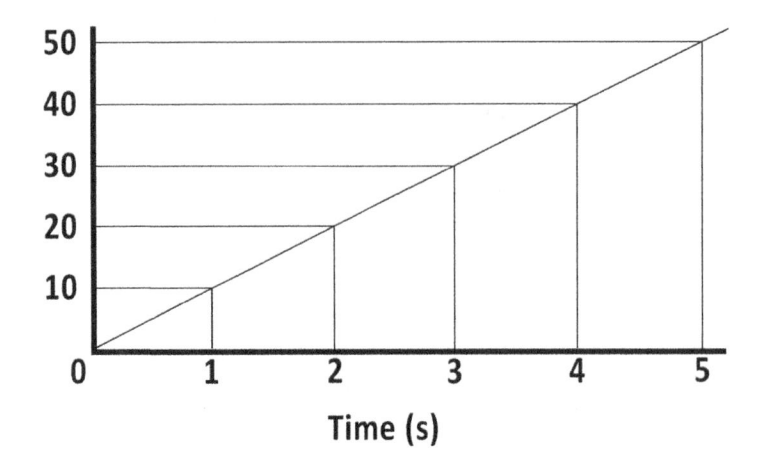

These pieces of information are used to determine past and future positions of the object being measured. A comparison of the movements of another object can determine trends in the positions of both objects.

The source of information from written dialogue, emails, or content can be used to determine the relevance of the material to the overall scope of the information. For example, an email from a company's marketing expert could contain more insight regarding a product's sales potential within a certain demographic compared to an email from a company's production manager. The source of the information determines the weight it should be given.

Manipulating Information from Multiple Sources to Solve Problems

Often data can be provided in a raw format that needs a bit of manipulation to find the desired answer. An example of this would be a table of data collected from an experiment or a survey taken from a sample. This type of data will often need to be rearranged so that comparisons can be made among the represented items. For example, the following information could be sorted in several ways to extrapolate specific information. The table could be sorted (as displayed) to determine the peak months for T-shirt purchases, or it could be re-sorted to determine the most purchased T-shirt size. Both pieces

Data Insights

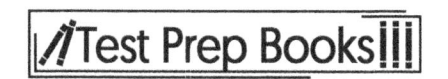

of information would come from the same data set, both would be important for production estimates, and both would require some manipulation of the information given.

	D	E	F
1	Payment	T-shirt Color	T-shirt Size
2	1 - Jan	Heather Gray	Large
3	1 - Jan	White	Large
4	4 - Jan	Dark Red	X - Large
5	5 - Jan	Dark Red	Medium
6	5 - Jan	Heather Gray	Large
7	5 - Jan	Dark Red	Medium
8	5 - Jan	Heather Gray	X - Large
9	6 - Jan	White	X - Large
10	6 - Jan	Dark Red	X - Large
11	7 - Jan	Heather Gray	Small
12	7 - Jan	Dark Red	Small
13	7 - Jan	Heather Gray	Small
14	7 - Jan	Heather Gray	Small
15	11 - Jan	Dark Red	Medium
16	11 - Jan	White	Medium
17	11 - Jan	Dark Red	Medium

In some cases, multiple pieces of information from various sources need to be used to assess a situation, solve a problem, or determine a sound course of action. For example, the following set of sources could be used to determine the best way for a small business to cater to its focus audience for advertising, sharing information, or simply networking. Each piece of information would need to be cross-referenced from one set of tables to the other to match up the best social media source for the desired small business goal.

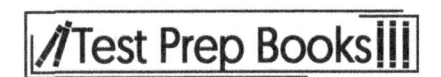

Social Media for Small Business Owners

Percentage of small businesses using the following in 2013

- 55 % Facebook
- 50 % Twitter
- 46 % LinkedIn
- 37 % None
- 30 % Pinterest
- 28 % Youtube
- 27 % Google+
- 16 % Instagram
- 10 % Blogs
- 6 % Foursquare

Percentage of small businesses using social media for:

- 75 % Business networking
- 52 % Keeping in touch with friends
- 21 % Political advocacy
- 6 % Other

Gathering information from multiple sources and then reapplying or manipulating it to make comparisons or estimates is the essence of what propels businesses. The importance of this can be seen in the cohesive branches of a business needing to communicate key pieces of information so the other branches can make decisions to further the company's overall goal. For instance, a T-shirt company needs to cross-reference production costs, availability of production products (such as textiles and dyes), implementation costs, employee costs and benefits, marketing strategies, and potential sales during both low and peak times. Additional promotions used for increasing sales could be observed and mapped onto existing data tables and manipulated to determine if the expense of the trial promotion produced enough profit to repeat.

Oftentimes, using information from multiple sources can assist with solving a basic problem. To hypothesize if a new idea would be profitable, it is recommended that some research be done to see if there are any types of similar productions, promotions, marketing, etc. This would require conducting a type of literature review and extracting any pertinent information that could be applied and manipulated to make estimates or predictions toward the idea being developed.

Data Insights

This requires a great deal of comparisons across multiple venues. When looking to make such comparisons, existing data is not always in the exact form necessary to draw a solid conclusion. Therefore, the research much be augmented by any predicted standard deviations or alternative results that could arise. This should include being able to make some predictions for plans a business might have involving the idea. For example, if a toy company wanted to produce a new toy that involved wheels, they would need to research similar toys that use the same type/size of wheels and decide if there were age restrictions for users, cost restrictions for production, durability restrictions for the use of the toy, and the overall aesthetics involved with the existing toys that use that type of wheel. This kind of information manipulation could aid in cutting costs, focusing marketing, and avoiding safety issues.

Two-Part Analysis

A few of the questions in the Data Analysis section will be two-part analysis questions. This requires test takers to solve complex problems that will have two answers. The questions may offer a short paragraph, a mathematical problem, or a mixture of both that test takers will evaluate and solve.

Here is an example of a two-part analysis question:

The quotient $\frac{x}{y}$ is a multiple of 7.

In the table below, choose the value of x and the value of y that are consistent with this statement. Make only one selection for x and one selection for y.

x	y	
O	O	72
O	O	119
O	O	1,296
O	O	13

The correct value for x is 1,176 and the correct value for y is 56 because $\frac{1176}{56} = 21$, which is a multiple of 7 because:

$$3 \times 7 = 21$$

Many two-part analysis questions will require test takers to try multiple answers to find out which one is right. Any of the other number combinations would have resulted in an answer that is not a multiple of 7, making them incorrect.

Take time to make sure that the correct answer is selected for the correct section, for example: the bubble under x should be filled at 1,176, and the bubble under y should be filled at 56. The opposite way would result in an answer of $\frac{1}{7}$, which is incorrect.

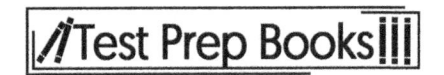

Table Analysis

One of the most common ways to express data is in a table. The primary reason for plugging data into a table is to make interpretation more convenient. It's much easier to look at the table than to analyze results in a narrative paragraph. When analyzing a table, pay close attention to the title, variables, and data.

Let's analyze a theoretical antibiotic study. The study has 6 groups, named A through F, and each group receives a different dose of medicine. The results of the study are listed in the table below.

Results of Antibiotic Studies		
Group	Dosage of Antibiotics in milligrams (mg)	Efficacy (% of participants cured)
A	0 mg	20%
B	20 mg	40%
C	40 mg	75%
D	60 mg	95%
E	80 mg	100%
F	100 mg	100%

Tables generally list the title immediately above the data. The title should succinctly explain what is listed below. Here, "Results of Antibiotic Studies" informs the audience that the data pertains to the results of a scientific study on antibiotics.

Identifying the variables at play is one of the most important parts of interpreting data. Remember, the independent variable is intentionally altered, and its change is independent of the other variables. Here, the dosage of antibiotics administered to the different groups is the independent variable. The study is intentionally manipulating the strength of the medicine to study the related results. Efficacy is the dependent variable since its results *depend* on a different variable, the dose of antibiotics. Generally, the independent variable will be listed before the dependent variable in tables.

Also, pay close attention to the variables' labels. Here, the dose is expressed in milligrams (mg) and efficacy in percentages (%). Keep an eye out for questions referencing data in a different unit measurement or questions asking for a raw number when only the percentage is listed.

Now that the nature of the study and variables at play have been identified, the data itself needs be interpreted. Group A did not receive any of the medicine. As discussed earlier, Group A is the control, as it reflects the amount of people cured in the same timeframe without medicine. It's important to see that efficacy positively correlates with the dosage of medicine. A question using this study might ask for the lowest dose of antibiotics to achieve 100% efficacy. Although Group E and Group F both achieve 100% efficacy, it's important to note that Group E reaches 100% with a lower dose.

Practice Quiz

Multi-Source Reasoning

Tab 1

Currently, the only health insurance plan offered to a certain company's employees is a zero-deductible plan, and its monthly premium is expensive for the employees. A zero deductible plan means that employees do not have to pay a minimum balance before insurance contributes to healthcare expenses. Currently, the insurance plan pays 90% of all covered medical costs. However, this plan comes at a high cost to the employees, and there will be more options given in open enrollment this year.

Tab 2: Email Announcement:

We are changing our company health insurance plan next year. Instead of the flat monthly fee of $500 for 90% coverage, there will be 4 different options for single employees. Details about family plans will be made available next week. The 4 options for single employees are:

- Single employees will keep the same level of coverage (90% of covered medical costs), and instead of paying $500 monthly for health insurance, they will have $250 taken out of each biweekly paycheck.

- A new option is a high deductible plan. With this plan, employees will have $50 taken out of each biweekly paycheck. Single employees will have a $5,000 deductible. After $5,000 is spent on medical costs, insurance will cover 90% of covered medical costs.

- A second new option is a different deductible. With this plan, single employees will have $100 taken out of each paycheck. Employees selecting this option will have a $3,000 deductible. After the deductible is spent on medical costs, insurance will cover 85% of covered medical costs.

- A final option involves a low deductible option. This plan involves $200 taken out of each paycheck, and single employees selecting this option will have a $1,000 deductible. After this amount is spent on medical costs, insurance will cover 80% of covered medical costs.

1. Based on the information provided, check either Yes or No for each of the following statements:

Yes	No	
○	○	The employees who select the same plan (with no deductible) will be paying the same yearly amount.
○	○	The high deductible plan will be selected the most often because it is the least expensive.
○	○	The low deductible plan will cost each single employee $5,200 a year.

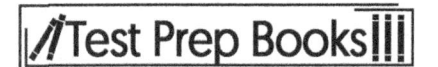

2. Based on the information provided, check either Yes or No for each of the following statements:

Yes	No	
○	○	An employee who estimates that she will have $10,000 in total covered medical costs next year should choose the high deductible plan.
○	○	An employee who anticipates no medical bills should choose the high deductible plan.
○	○	An employee who estimates that he will have $100,000 in total covered medical costs next year should choose the high deductible plan.

Graphics Interpretation

This graph shows the relation between real house prices and Freddie Mac Survey mortgage rates between January 1976 and January 2014.

Real House Prices and Mortgage Rates

Data Insights

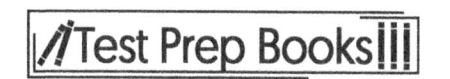

Based on of the information in the graph, fill in the blanks:

3. _____ maintains the largest consistent discrepancy between the real house prices and the survey house prices.
   a. January 1981–January 1983
   b. January 1980–January 1982
   c. January 1998–January 2000
   d. January 2006–January 2008

The real house price rises above the survey house price for the first time in _____.
   a. January 1995
   b. January 1986
   c. January 1989

Two-Part Analysis

4. Max can complete an analysis in 5 hours, while Dottie can compete the same analysis in 3 hours. Select a value for the time it would take them to finish the analysis if they worked together and by what difference this would be faster than Dottie's time.

Make one selection for each column:

Time Together	Difference	
○	○	a. 1.625
○	○	b. 1.875
○	○	c. 1.125
○	○	d. 0.625

Data Sufficiency

5. Of the 804 graduating seniors, a portion are going on to salaried positions after college. Approximately $\frac{1}{4}$ of those positions will be in state. What is the closest estimate for how many graduates taking salaried positions will be staying in state?

   1) $\frac{2}{5}$ of the 804 are going on to salaried positions.

   2) $\frac{3}{4}$ of the salaried positions are out of state.

   a. Statement (1) ALONE is sufficient, but statement (2) alone is not sufficient to answer the question asked.
   b. Statement (2) ALONE is sufficient, but statement (1) alone is not sufficient to answer the question asked.
   c. BOTH statements (1) and (2) TOGETHER are sufficient to answer the question asked, but NEITHER statement ALONE is sufficient to answer the question asked.
   d. EACH statement ALONE is sufficient to answer the question asked.
   e. Statements (1) and (2) TOGETHER are NOT sufficient to answer the question asked, and additional data specific to the problem are needed.

Table Analysis

U.S. Internet Sales in 2017 of the ABC Cable Company.

		Package Selection		
		Basic Package	Deluxe Package	Extra Deluxe Package
Region	Northeast	40.4	55.1	20.1
	Midwest	45.2	60.3	15.8
	South	34.1	41.2	23.1
	West	16.1	22.3	13.2

Note: All numbers above are in thousands.

6. Check either True or False for each of the following statements:

True	False	
○	○	The average number of basic packages sold was 135,800.
○	○	The percentage of packages sold that were not basic was approximately 35%.
○	○	The region with the largest number of internet sales for the ABC Cable Company was the Midwest.

Answer Explanations

Multi-Source Reasoning

1. NO: The employees in the previous year pay $500 monthly, which totals $6,000 per year. Next year, the employees will pay $250 biweekly, which totals $6,500.

NO: The other plans might make more sense for some employees who anticipate having high medical bills.

YES: The low deductible plan costs $200 biweekly, which totals $5,200 per year.

2. NO: The high deductible plan will cost the employee $6,800 ($1300 in premiums plus $5,000 toward the deductible and 10% of costs after deductible, which is $500). The middle deductible plan will cost the employee $6,650 ($2600 in premiums plus $3,000 toward the deductible and 15% of costs after deductible, which is $1,050).

YES: An employee who projects no medical costs should choose the plan with the lowest premium, and that is the high deductible plan, which costs the employee $1,300 a year.

YES: The high deductible plan will cost the employee $16,300, which is the lowest cost. This includes the $1,300 paid toward the premium, $5,000 toward the deductible, and 10% of $100,000, which equals $10,000 paid toward costs after the deductible.

Graphics Interpretation

3. D, C: For the first sentence, while all choices (*A, B, C,* and *D*) contain large spikes in discrepancies between the real house prices and the survey house prices, January 2006 to January 2008 covers the largest window of discrepancies.

For the second sentence, if you follow the line of survey house prices, it is below the real house price until approximately January of 1989 on the chart.

Two-Part Analysis

4. Time Together is B and Difference is C: The method of calculating their combined analysis time is as follows:

$$\frac{1}{5} + \frac{1}{3} = \frac{1}{x}$$

$$\frac{15x}{1}\left(\frac{1}{5} + \frac{1}{3}\right) = \frac{15x}{1}\left(\frac{1}{x}\right)$$

$$3x + 5x = 15$$

$$8x = 15$$

$$x = \frac{15}{8} = 1.875$$

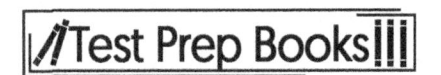

The difference would be calculated as follows:

$$3 - 1.875 = 1.125$$

Data Sufficiency

5. A: Only statement 1 has information necessary to complete the calculations as follows:

$$\frac{2}{5}(804) = 321.6$$

$$\frac{1}{4}(321.6) = 80.4$$

$$80 \text{ positions}$$

Table Analysis

6. FALSE: The total number of basic packages sold was 135,800. However, dividing this amount by 4 results in an average of 33,950.

FALSE: The total number of non-basic packages sold was 251,100, and the total number of packages sold was 386,900, which is a percentage of 65%.

TRUE: The region with the largest number of internet sales for the ABC Cable Company was the Midwest. Totaling up the number of packages for each region results in the largest total for the Midwest region, 121,300 packages.

GMAT Practice Test #1

Quantitative Reasoning

1. Johnny earns $2,334.50 from his job each month. He pays $1,437 for monthly expenses and saves the rest. Johnny is planning a vacation in 3 months that he estimates will cost $1,750 total. How much will Johnny have left over from 3 months of saving once he pays for his vacation?
    a. $948.50
    b. $584.50
    c. $852.50
    d. $942.50
    e. $952.50

2. Keith's bakery had 252 customers go through its doors last week. This week, that number increased to 378. Express this increase as a percentage.
    a. 26%
    b. 50%
    c. 35%
    d. 12%
    e. 28%

3. If 40% of y is 24, then y is what percent of 120?
    a. 30%
    b. 40%
    c. 50%
    d. 60%
    e. 70%

4. The phone bill is calculated each month using the equation $c = 50g + 75$. The cost of the phone bill per month is represented by c, and g represents the gigabytes of data used that month. What is the value and interpretation of the slope of this equation?
    a. 75 dollars per day
    b. 75 gigabytes per day
    c. 50 dollars per day
    d. 50 dollars per gigabyte
    e. 25 dollars per day

5. The ratio of fruit to vegetables at a grocery store is 5: 3. If the total number of produce items (fruits and vegetables) is 120, how many vegetables are in the store?
    a. 45
    b. 75
    c. 100
    d. 50
    e. 30

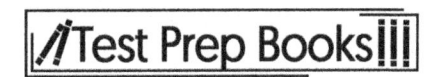

6. If $\sqrt[3]{m} = 2$ and $m = \sqrt{n}$, what is the value of n?
   a. 36
   b. 2
   c. 16
   d. 8
   e. 64

7. A bag contains 30 marbles. 8 are blue, 10 are red, and 12 are purple. If two marbles are selected at random without replacement, what is the probability that one marble will be purple and the other will be blue?
   a. $\frac{24}{225}$
   b. $\frac{2}{3}$
   c. $\frac{32}{145}$
   d. $\frac{48}{435}$
   e. $\frac{4}{15}$

8. Kristy wants to have an average score of at least 75 on her 5 math tests this year. On the first 4 tests, she obtained an average score of 73. Let x be equal to the score she must achieve on her last test. Which of the following is the correct inequality?
   a. $x < 100$
   b. $x \geq 83$
   c. $70 \leq x \leq 80$
   d. $x < 75.5$
   e. $x \geq 76$

9. x and y are numbers such that when y is divided by x, the remainder is 9. It is also true that $\frac{y}{x} = 8.4$. What is the value of x?
   a. 7.5
   b. 22
   c. 75.6
   d. 52
   e. 22.5

10. Let x be an integer that is negative and let y be an integer that is positive. Which of the following quantities will always produce a positive integer?
    a. $xy + x$
    b. $y^x + y$
    c. $x^y - y$
    d. xy^2
    e. $x + y$

GMAT Practice Test #1

11. A magazine salesperson needs to average 20 subscriptions an hour to make quota. However, to obtain a bonus each day, their average must be 20% higher than the minimum necessary to make quota. So far today, the salesperson's hourly sales have been 16, 14, 18, 20, 16, and 28. If their shift is 8 hours long, what must their average sales be for the rest of the day in order to earn a bonus?
    a. 20
    b. 40
    c. 60
    d. 80
    e. 100

12. Compute the following: $\left(\frac{1}{2}-\frac{1}{5}\right)+\left(\frac{1}{3}+\frac{1}{5}\right)-\left(\frac{1}{6}+\frac{1}{4}\right)+\left(\frac{1}{3}+\frac{1}{7}\right)$
    a. $\frac{27}{28}$
    b. $\frac{11}{12}$
    c. $\frac{25}{28}$
    d. $\frac{9}{11}$
    e. $\frac{22}{51}$

13. 5 classrooms are participating in the end-of-the-year sports tournament. They compete in various events and will be ranked from 1st to 5th place at the end of the tournament. Only 1st through 3rd places will receive trophies. How many different ways can there be in the ordering of trophies if one of the classes (which placed first last year) can no longer place first again?
    a. 120
    b. 60
    c. 12
    d. 8
    e. 48

14. Which of the following is closest to $\sqrt{\frac{87.6(2,580)}{16.2^2}}$?
    a. 20
    b. 30
    c. 40
    d. 50
    e. 60

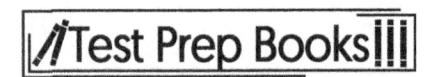

15. A gas tank is $\frac{1}{4}$ full. x gallons of gas were added to the tank, which filled the tank to $\frac{7}{8}$ of its capacity. What is the capacity of the gas tank in gallons?
   a. $\frac{3}{5}x$
   b. $\frac{1}{8}x$
   c. $\frac{8}{5}x$
   d. $\frac{5}{8}x$
   e. $\frac{5}{3}x$

16. Let x be an integer such that $4 < x < 200$. For how many of these values of x is $\frac{x}{4}$ equal to a prime number squared?
   a. 2
   b. 3
   c. 4
   d. 5
   e. 6

17. 70% of a real estate company's agents work full time. There are 560 more full-time agents than part-time agents. How many total agents does the company have?
   a. 1400
   b. 980
   c. 420
   d. 2400
   e. 640

18. The arithmetic mean for a set of numbers is 7.2. The standard deviation for the same set of numbers is 3.15. Which of the following numbers lies more than 3 standard deviations away from the mean?
   a. -2
   b. -3
   c. 15
   d. 16
   e. 11

GMAT Practice Test #1

19. Given the following function, what is the value of $f(-1)$?

$$f(x) = \begin{cases} 5|x|, x < -1 \\ -5|x|, -1 \leq x \leq 1 \\ \frac{-1}{5}|x|, x \geq 1 \end{cases}$$

a. $\frac{1}{5}$

b. 5

c. -5

d. $\frac{-1}{5}$

e. 1

20. Katie and Joe have been asked to present at a conference. There are 8 women and 8 men at the conference, and one woman and one man are selected to present on Monday. What is the probability that neither Katie nor Joe will present on Monday?

a. $\frac{1}{4}$

b. $\frac{1}{64}$

c. $\frac{1}{32}$

d. $\frac{7}{8}$

e. $\frac{63}{64}$

21. Let $\frac{1}{x} = 4\frac{1}{3}$. Find the value of $\left(\frac{2}{x+3}\right)^2$.

a. $\frac{169}{441}$

b. $\frac{676}{441}$

c. $\frac{169}{1764}$

d. $\frac{169}{221}$

e. $\frac{36}{256}$

65

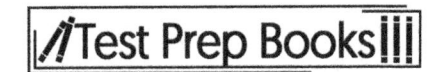

Verbal Reasoning

Reading Comprehension

Questions 1–4 are based on the following passage:

Cellular respiration is one of the fundamental biochemical processes essential for life. The primary purpose of this process is to convert glucose and oxygen into energy that the cell can use—energy in the form of a molecule called adenosine triphosphate (ATP). This energy is critical for driving a variety of cellular functions, including active transport, protein synthesis, and muscle contraction. All of these functions are necessary for the survival of cells and thus for the survival of the organism itself.

The cellular respiration process begins with glycolysis, which occurs in the cell's cytoplasm and entails the breakdown of a glucose molecule into two molecules of pyruvate. This step generates a small amount of ATP and NADH (nicotinamide adenine dinucleotide), an energy carrier. The pyruvate then enters the mitochondria, where it undergoes pyruvate oxidation. In this step, each pyruvate is converted into acetyl-CoA, releasing carbon dioxide and producing additional NADH.

The acetyl-CoA then enters the citric acid cycle, also known as the Krebs cycle, which consists of a series of chemical reactions that take place within the mitochondrial matrix. During this cycle, acetyl-CoA is further broken down, producing ATP, NADH, and $FADH_2$ (all of which are crucial to further energy production), while carbon dioxide is released as a byproduct.

The final stage, oxidative phosphorylation, occurs in the inner mitochondrial membrane and utilizes the electron transport chain and chemiosmosis to harness energy. NADH and $FADH_2$ give up electrons to the electron transport chain, which releases energy to create a proton gradient across the membrane. The proton gradient is then used in chemiosmosis to produce ATP. Oxygen acts as the final electron acceptor, combining with the existing protons and electrons to form water.

Beyond the creation of energy, cellular respiration also manages the byproducts from these processes—primarily carbon dioxide and water—which are expelled from the cell and then from the organism entirely. Thus, cellular respiration not only provides energy but also helps maintain cellular balance by removing metabolic waste.

1. Which of the following accurately describes what the passage is primarily concerned with?
    a. Explaining the various steps that take place during cellular respiration and why they are important
    b. Questioning what happens to the byproducts created during the process of cellular respiration
    c. Analyzing how cellular respiration impacts the growth rates of various types of organisms, such as plants
    d. Discussing the inefficiency of the process that cells go through in order to generate energy for themselves

2. Based on the passage, which of the following is a byproduct of both pyruvate oxidation and the citric acid cycle?
    a. Oxygen
    b. Water
    c. Carbon dioxide
    d. ATP

3. According to the passage, which of the following occurs during the glycolysis stage?
    a. The byproducts carbon dioxide and water are expelled from the cells.
    b. A glucose molecule is broken down into two molecules of pyruvate.
    c. Electrons are used to create an electron transport chain and a proton gradient.
    d. Acetyl-CoA is broken down into ATP, NADH, and $FADH_2$.

4. Which of the following scenarios serves as an appropriate analogy for the function of the proton gradient in producing ATP?
    a. A library worker sorting books onto various shelves according to their size and shape
    b. A banker counting money starting with the smallest bills before working up to the largest
    c. A power plant burning fuel to generate electricity for a city
    d. A dam that uses multiple turbines in order to generate electricity

Questions 5–7 are based on the following passage:

The invention of the steam engine during the Industrial Revolution marked a pivotal point in history, dramatically changing various industries, transportation, and society. James Watt's 1765 version of the steam engine became essential for powering factories and expanding railways, marking a new era of technological advancement.

Prior to the steam engine, industries such as textiles and mining relied on manual labor, animals, or water-powered mills. These energy sources were limited in efficiency and restricted production to locations near water bodies. The steam engine's creation provided a consistent and powerful energy source that was not dependent on geographical location and thus allowed factories to be built in more advantageous locations, closer to markets as well as to their raw materials.

For the average person, the most significant impact of the steam engine was seen in transportation. By the early 19th century, steam-powered trains and ships had revolutionized travel. Railroads were used to transport goods and people over long distances at speeds previously unimaginable, spurring trade and helping develop new industries and markets. Steamships shortened travel time across oceans, enhancing global trade and connecting distant regions in ways that were once impossible. The tourist industry developed in new ways as more people were able to travel the country and abroad.

5. Which of the following can be inferred about life before the steam engine?
    a. People traveled easily to far-away destinations to buy things they did not have at home.
    b. Factories were dependent on energy generated by natural sources such as water and animals.
    c. Global trade was extensive and people around the world were connected.
    d. Factories were located near mountains so that the workers could use local stone and wood.

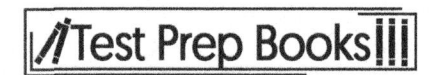

6. According to the passage, which industries benefited the most from the invention of steam-powered transportation?
   a. Tourism and shipping
   b. Agriculture and logging
   c. Telecommunication and banking
   d. Textiles and retail

7. What was the steam engine's main impact on factories?
   a. Factories were forced to shut down due to the new preference for global trade.
   b. Factory workers were forced to find other jobs as they were replaced by steam engines.
   c. Factories continued to rely on their proximity to a water source.
   d. Factories could be built closer to markets and raw materials.

Questions 8–10 are based on the following passage:

Geothermal and solar energy are two renewable power sources that each have advantages and challenges. They are both solid options for reducing the global reliance on fossil fuels; however, they operate differently and should be used in different situations.

Geothermal energy is heat energy that is found within the earth's interior. Geothermal energy is extracted by tapping into underground reservoirs of steam or hot water, which are typically located near volcanoes or tectonic activity. The energy from this heat is then used to generate electricity. Geothermal electricity generation does not consume a finite resource in a given area but relies instead on a continuous heat source, making it a reliable source of energy. It is also not dependent on the weather or time of day like other renewable energy sources. However, due to the difficulty of finding locations where geothermal energy plants would have access to these heat sources, geothermal energy is not a widespread renewable energy source option.

Solar technologies use photovoltaic cells or solar thermal systems to generate electricity by harnessing solar energy from sunlight. Sunlight reaches the vast majority of the earth year round, so solar power is considered a universally available energy source. However, harnessing solar power can only occur during daytime hours and is severely limited by poor weather, so the energy must be stored in batteries to ensure a steady supply of power regardless of the sun's availability.

8. What is the primary purpose of this passage?
   a. To explain the importance of replacing fossil fuels with renewable energy
   b. To describe the financial savings that come with investing in renewable energy
   c. To argue that geothermal energy is a better option than solar energy
   d. To compare the advantages and challenges of geothermal and solar energy

GMAT Practice Test #1

9. The author most likely mentions geographical requirements for geothermal energy plants for what reason?
    a. To point out why geothermal electricity generation is so expensive to implement
    b. To argue that geothermal energy is not a practical energy source and should not be used
    c. To explain one of the limitations for geothermal energy being relied upon globally
    d. To show that solar energy is a superior energy source since it can be used anywhere

10. According to the information provided in the passage, which of the following would be the best location for a geothermal power plant?
    a. A desert with extreme temperatures
    b. A windy area with lots of sunlight
    c. A rainy area with volcanic activity
    d. A coastline with underground oil reservoirs

Questions 11–13 are based on the following passage:

Price elasticity of demand is the measure of the responsiveness of the quantity demanded to a change in price for a particular product or service. This economic concept is critical to understanding consumer and market behavior. Price elasticity is calculated by dividing the percentage change in quantity demanded by the percentage change in price. Based on this number, the demand for the product or service can be classified as elastic, inelastic, or unitary elastic.

Elastic demand, which has a price elasticity that is greater than 1, responds more strongly to price changes such that a relatively small change in price leads to a relatively large change in the quantity demanded. This is generally seen with non-essential or luxury goods. Since these goods and services are not necessary, consumers are generally more sensitive to price changes. For example, if an expensive handbag or high-end television were to increase in price, the demand would most likely decrease significantly.

Inelastic demand, which has a price elasticity that is less than 1, exhibits a relatively weak response to price changes such that the change in price of an item has little effect on the quantity demanded. This generally applies to items that are essential as consumers must buy them regardless of their price. Medication and food items often increase in price, yet their demand stays relatively stable. Businesses consider this concept when pricing items since they wish to maximize profits. Policymakers take this into account in order to ensure that consumers are not being taken advantage of based on this concept.

11. Why does the passage most likely mention non-essential and luxury goods?
    a. To suggest that luxury goods are more important to the economy than essential goods
    b. To show how demand can be dependent on the price of certain types of goods and services
    c. To argue that consumers should not purchase luxury goods due to their high price elasticity
    d. To provide context for how socioeconomic standing affects people's reactions to price increases

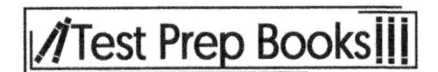

12. Which of the following scenarios demonstrates elastic demand according to the information provided in the passage?
    a. A common medication has decreased in price, but its demand has stayed the same.
    b. The cost of motorcycles has decreased slightly, which leads to a small increase in demand.
    c. A luxury car's price increases slightly, leading to a significant decrease in the number of cars sold.
    d. Gasoline has increased in price and has also seen an increase in demand.

13. Based on this passage, it can be inferred that businesses concern themselves with price elasticity of demand for what reason?
    a. To protect buyers from paying exorbitant prices on essential goods
    b. To determine how to reach maximum profits
    c. To reduce the cost of production for their goods
    d. To ensure that buyers maintain brand loyalty despite price changes

Critical Reasoning

14. Julia joined Michael Scott Paperless Company, a small New York based tech start-up company, last month. Michael Scott Paperless recently received a valuation of ten million dollars. Julia is clearly the reason for the valuation.
Which of the following statements, if true, most weakens the argument?
    a. Michael Scott Paperless Company released an extremely popular mobile application shortly before hiring Julia.
    b. Michael Scott Paperless Company is wildly overvalued.
    c. Julia is an expert in her field.
    d. Julia only started working two weeks before the valuation.
    e. Julia completed two important projects during her first month with the company.

15. Advertisement: Cigarettes are deadly. Hundreds of thousands of people die every year from smoking-related causes, such as lung cancer or heart disease. The science is clear—smoking a pack per day for years will shorten one's life. Sitting in a room where someone is smoking might as well be a gas chamber in terms of damage to long-term health.
Which one of the following best describes the flaw in the author's reasoning?
    a. The advertisement confuses cause and effect.
    b. The advertisement uses overly broad generalization.
    c. The advertisement draws an unjustified analogy.
    d. The advertisement relies on shoddy science.
    e. The advertisement makes an unreasonable logical leap.

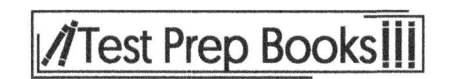

16. Blue Zones are regions where people live notably longer lives. Areas like Okinawa and Sardinia commonly have residents who live to be over 90 years of age. Researchers attribute this longevity to a combination of factors, which may include a plant-based diet, routine physical activity, and strong community relationships. These elements, rather than genetics, are considered key contributors to the low rates of disease and to the extended life expectancies seen in Blue Zones.

Which of the following would weaken the argument being made about the factors contributing to longer life expectancies in Blue Zones?
   a. Individuals within Blue Zones typically work manual labor jobs at a similar rate to those living outside of Blue Zones.
   b. People who eat plant-based diets in other regions do not experience the same extended life expectancy as those living within Blue Zones.
   c. Introducing animal products and processed foods into a Blue Zone does not seem to dramatically alter the life expectancy of residents.
   d. Recent studies have shown that those native to Blue Zones have genetic traits making them more resistant to chronic disease and illness.
   e. The life expectancy of young individuals who move to a Blue Zone increases to approximately match that of those who were born there.

17. Outdoor classrooms offer significant benefits by enhancing student learning and well-being. Exposure to nature reduces stress and improves focus while hands-on, real-world learning opportunities enrich subjects like science and geography. Additionally, outdoor environments encourage physical activity, supporting both health and cognitive development. These are all key factors in successful education for young students and can all lead to higher educational performance.

Which of the following would best strengthen the argument made regarding the impact of outdoor classrooms on educational performance?
   a. Outdoor classrooms are most beneficial in the warmer months of the year.
   b. Schools that feature outdoor classrooms have higher standardized test scores in science-related subjects than schools that do not feature outdoor classrooms.
   c. Field trips that take place outdoors are shown to enhance the knowledge retention of students who participate.
   d. Research has shown that outdoor learning leads to positive benefits for the mental and physical health of students.
   e. Outdoor extracurricular school activities, such as sports, are shown to improve critical-thinking and problem-solving skills in students.

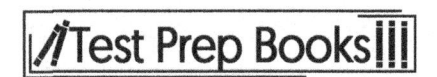

18. Over the past decade, bee populations have declined considerably, leading to the claim that pesticides are the primary cause of this decline. However, studies have shown that factors such as habitat loss and climate change have been equally significant, countering the claim. This is evidenced by a continued decline in bee populations even in areas that have banned pesticides.

Which of the following is an assumption upon which the counterclaim depends?
   a. Bee populations in areas without banned pesticides can occasionally see short-term increases depending on the type of pesticide being used.
   b. The effects of climate change can be hard to identify and measure in a quantifiable manner unlike the use of pesticides, which can be easily tracked.
   c. Pesticides are regulated more strictly than other variables such as habitat loss in regions where bees are declining in numbers.
   d. Bee populations in areas that have discontinued pesticide use would have stabilized if pesticides were the primary factor in their decline.
   e. Habitat conservation has not been enough to improve bee populations in areas with heavy pesticide use.

19. It has long been believed that there is a connection between physical exercise and cognitive function. One recent study showed that individuals who exercised 30 minutes per day performed better on memory tests than individuals who did not exercise at all. Therefore, the best way to improve one's memory is to exercise at least 30 minutes per day.

Which of the following would best weaken this argument?
   a. A study found that people who exercise regularly also tend to eat a balanced diet, which improves health.
   b. A survey showed that individuals who regularly perform highly on memory tests are more likely to have poor mental health.
   c. Research shows that people who exercise for 30 minutes per day improve on memory tests by an equal measure as those who meditate for 30 minutes per day.
   d. Studies show that individuals who exercise for 30 minutes per day see greater improvements on memory tests than individuals for exercise for 2 hours once per week.
   e. Further testing showed that the memory improvement from exercising daily was short term and diminished quickly with even a few days of inconsistent exercise.

20. In order to increase efficiency, a company is considering project management software to automate tasks and provide real-time updates. However, a supervisor suggests assigning the tasks to a single employee instead. They argue that having one person handle these tasks allows for more flexibility in managing unique situations, while software might be too rigid and less adaptable to sudden changes. Which of the following would best strengthen the supervisor's argument?
   a. Studies have shown that companies that rely on software for project management often experience delays during the adjustment process.
   b. A trial run with a similar software at a different company showed that the company had 30 percent more errors related to updates and emails than when they had a dedicated employee doing the same job.
   c. Top 500 companies have discovered that task automation improves efficiency but that employees may feel micromanaged.
   d. Financial experts argue that implementing this type of software can save companies hundreds of thousands of dollars that would otherwise be spent on dedicated employees.
   e. Employees from other departments have reported that a combination of their work and the software's work yields the best results in terms of productivity.

21. City planners have reviewed a study that showed that cities with extensive public transportation systems have less traffic congestion than cities with limited public transportation. Therefore, they have concluded that all of the traffic problems within the city would be resolved if they expand the city's public transportation system.
Which of the following, if true, would weaken the city planners' argument?
   a. Data from cities with limited public transportation show an increase in traffic congestion from year to year.
   b. Cities that implement extensive public transportation systems often experience economic growth.
   c. Surveys show that residents of cities often do not want public transportation to be expanded due to the tax increases it would bring.
   d. Results from a poll showed that the majority of city residents would not be able to utilize the public transportation system often since many of their workplaces are outside of the city.
   e. Cities with that expand their public transportation systems often see increases in crime rates, notably at bus stops, subway stations, etc.

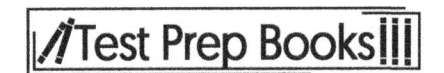

22. Literacy programs in early childhood can significantly improve reading skills. The National Institute for Literacy claims that children who participated in literacy interventions at a preschool age showed higher levels of reading proficiency by the third grade compared to children who did not. For this reason, public programs run by libraries are the easiest way for families to improve the literacy skills of their young children.

Which of the following would best weaken the argument about library-run literacy programs being the easiest way to improve children's literacy skills?
   a. Research indicates that after-school programs can also be successful in raising literacy rates for children who attend.
   b. Many families use libraries to obtain free books to read to children who are too young for school, which is shown to improve literacy as they get older.
   c. Libraries often struggle to find funding for literacy programs and need the support of the community to fund them.
   d. Students with socioeconomic disadvantages do not have easy access to library programs as their parents are generally working long hours and they have no transportation.
   e. Private one-on-one tutoring programs have been shown to improve literacy skills in students performing below their grade level expectations.

23. Alex is a young professional who has embraced digital payment systems to streamline his daily financial activity. He uses mobile payment apps to eliminate his need to carry cash and to speed up his transactions. Alex argues that digital payment technology is more convenient and secure than traditional methods of payment such as cash and checks and thus those options should no longer be available.

Which of the following weakens the argument for digital payment systems?
   a. Research shows that the majority of consumers prefer using cash for small purchases under ten dollars.
   b. Surveys show that consumers feel wary about digital payment options due to their lack of understanding about how the software works.
   c. Studies show that digital payment options reduce transaction times by 60 percent and improve consumer satisfaction.
   d. Digital payment apps occasionally experience outages, and it can take hours to restore service.
   e. Multiple security features are available for digital payment systems that protect consumers' personal and payment information.

Data Insights

Multi-Source Reasoning

Set 1

Tab 1

Over the past 10 years, San Francisco has been striving to improve the city and increase tourism. The following data shows associated costs the city has incurred for improvements over this time.

2014	2015	2016	2017	2018	2019	2020	2021	2022	2023
$25,250	$30,500	$32,100	$27,025	$31,750	$36,075	$45,000	$44,250	$48,275	$51,500

Tab 2

Tourists (in Millions) in San Francisco per Year									
2014	2015	2016	2017	2018	2019	2020	2021	2022	2023
0.85	1.0	1.2	1.4	1.7	2.1	2.6	3.5	4.2	4.8

Tab 3

Increased focus on improving infrastructure, marketing strategies, public transportation, and hotels was a major factor in recent years. Additionally, new public attractions were a major focus of marketing campaigns centered around promoting tourism in order to increase revenue for the city as a whole. Each year, the percentage of funding that each of these areas received during the city's campaign to increase tourism was as follows:

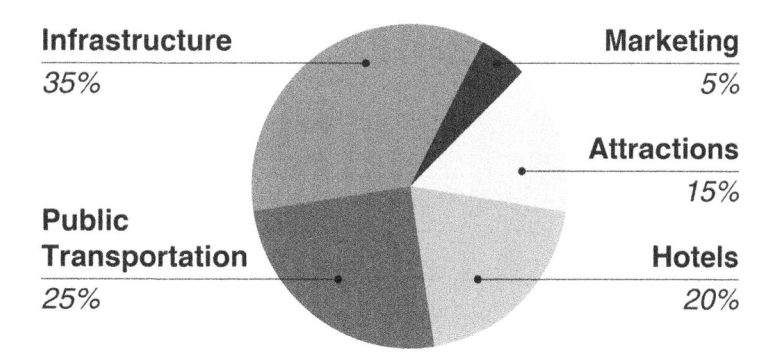

- Infrastructure 35%
- Marketing 5%
- Attractions 15%
- Hotels 20%
- Public Transportation 25%

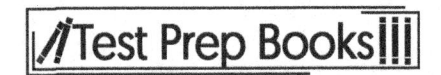

1. Between 2019 and 2023, what was the average annual increase in the number of tourists in San Francisco (in millions)?
    a. 0.425
    b. 0.585
    c. 0.675
    d. 0.750
    e. 0.825

2. Check either Yes or No for each of the following statements:

Yes	No	
○	○	In 2017, the number of tourists was at least 20% less than in 2020.
○	○	The amount spent on infrastructure between 2016 and 2019 was more than the average spent on all improvements from 2020 to 2022.
○	○	Out of the strategies implemented by the city to improve tourism, improving public transportation, infrastructure, and hotels accounted for more than 85% of all costs.

3. Which of the following statements about San Francisco's campaign to improve tourism over the past ten years are true?

   I. The average cost of improvements over the last ten years was greater than $36,500.

   II. $4,575 was spent on improving city attractions in 2015.

   III. The median number of tourists was 1.9.

   IV. The average annual increase in tourists between 2014 and 2021 was 0.41 million.

   V. The total amount spent on public transportation was $18,586.25 more than the total amount spent on hotels.

    a. I, II, IV
    b. II, III, V
    c. II, III, IV, V
    d. I, II, III, V
    e. All of the above

Set 2
Tab 1

A survey of the population in Charlotte, NC, found that 15% of the population has a high school diploma, 35% of the population has a bachelor's degree, 30% has a master's degree, 10% has a doctorate, and 10% never finished high school. Additionally, 64.5% of the population are homeowners. All of these statistics have remained the same for the past decade. Furthermore, 9.4% of non-homeowners in 2024 owned a home at some point in the past.

Tab 2

Housing costs have been rising over the past 10 years. Additionally, based on citywide data, the prices that renters pay for rental homes rose 2.7% each year from 2015 through 2020, and they have risen 4.5% each year since then. The average cost of a rental in 2024 is $2,400 per month. The following data represents average house prices in Charlotte, NC:

Year	Average House Price
2015	$325,609
2016	$355,622
2017	$362,824
2018	$375,075
2019	$387,550
2020	$400,075
2021	$410,125
2022	$425,507
2023	$450,025
2024	$475,504

Tab 3

The population of Charlotte, NC, has seen growth over the past decade due to various improvements the city has made, including improvements in public transportation, building more hotels, lowering crime rates, and raising the employment rate. Additionally, the city is attempting to prevent homeowners from losing their homes by implementing house payment relief programs, and it is also putting into effect a program to incentivize homebuying by giving tax breaks to people buying houses. The following data represents Charlotte's population over the course of the last 10 years:

Year	Total Population
2015	832,194
2016	847,008
2017	855,091
2018	862,034
2019	875,102
2020	882,099
2021	893,465
2022	902,405
2023	911,907
2024	920,024

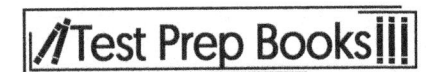

4. If population growth continues at the same rate as it did between 2023 and 2024 and the percentage of people with a master's degree increases by 2% each year, how many people will have a master's degree in 2027?
   a. 340,131
   b. 364,982
   c. 395,741
   d. 401,906
   e. 422,198

5. Check either Yes or No for each of the following statements:

Yes	No	
○	○	The average annual increase in the total number of people with a master's degree between 2015 and 2021 was more than the population increase between 2016 and 2017.
○	○	The number of people who did not own homes in 2018 was greater than the total population increase between 2015 and 2024.
○	○	In the coming years, the percentage of citizens who own homes is likely to be higher than 64.5%.

6. Given the information provided, which of the following statements would be considered accurate?

   I. The average percentage by which the population increased between 2020 and 2024 was greater than the average percentage by which the cost of houses rose between 2018 and 2022.

   II. If the population rises by the same percentage from 2024 to 2025 as it did from 2023 to 2024, the number of people who will not own homes in 2025 will be 304,262.

   III. The average number of people who owned homes and had a bachelor's degree between 2017 and 2020 was greater than the average number of people who did not own homes with a master's degree between 2016 and 2021.

   IV. The average percent increase in the average cost of houses between 2015 and 2020 was less than that between 2020 and 2024.

   V. In 2024, the average cost of a rental per month is less than 1% of the average price of a house.

   a. I, III, V
   b. II, IV
   c. V
   d. III, IV, V
   e. All of the above

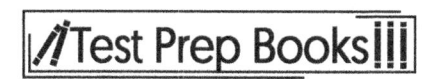

Graphics Interpretation

7. The following graph represents a comparison of the production output of 4 small appliance factories in each quarter of each year between 2021 and 2023.

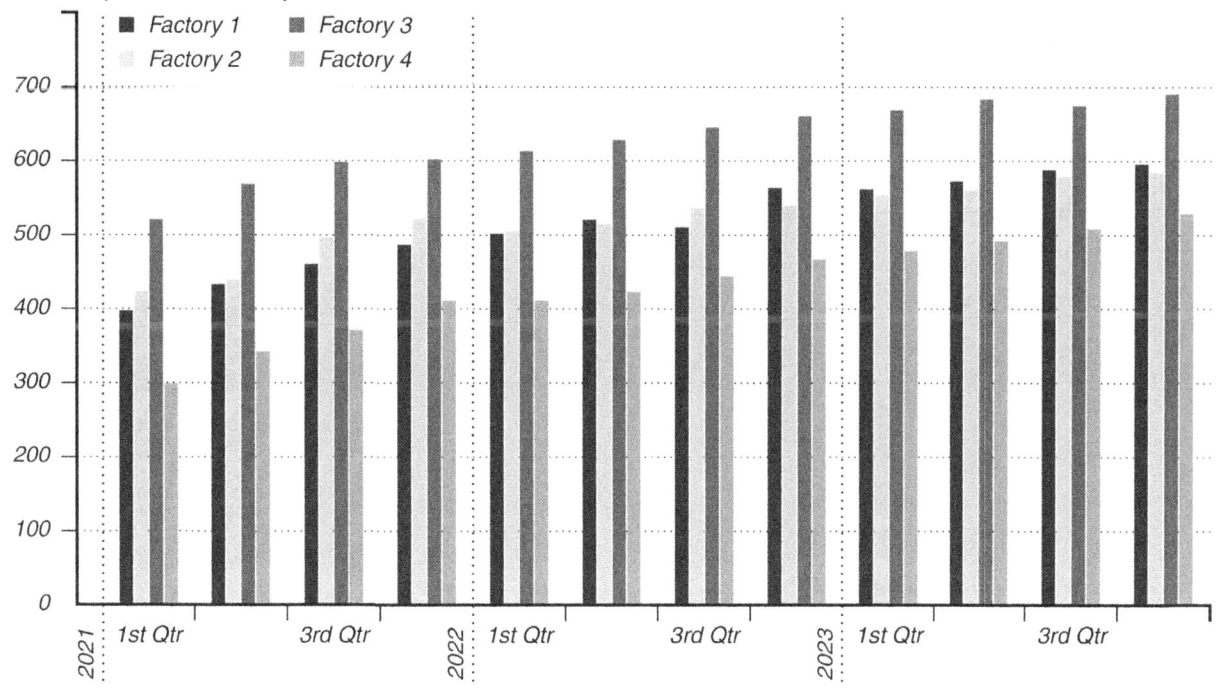

Based on of the information in the graph, fill in the blanks:

The percent increase in production output for Factory 2 between quarters 1 and 3 in 2021 was
_____.

   a. 10.2%
   b. 17.6%
   c. 19.8%
   d. 21.4%

The last factory to have an increase of 100 from its production during the first quarter of 2021 was
_____.

   a. Factory 1
   b. Factory 2
   c. Factory 3
   d. Factory 4

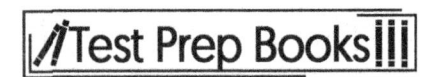

8. The following is a graph of the market shares, profit margins, and revenue (in millions) for 10 cybersecurity companies this year:

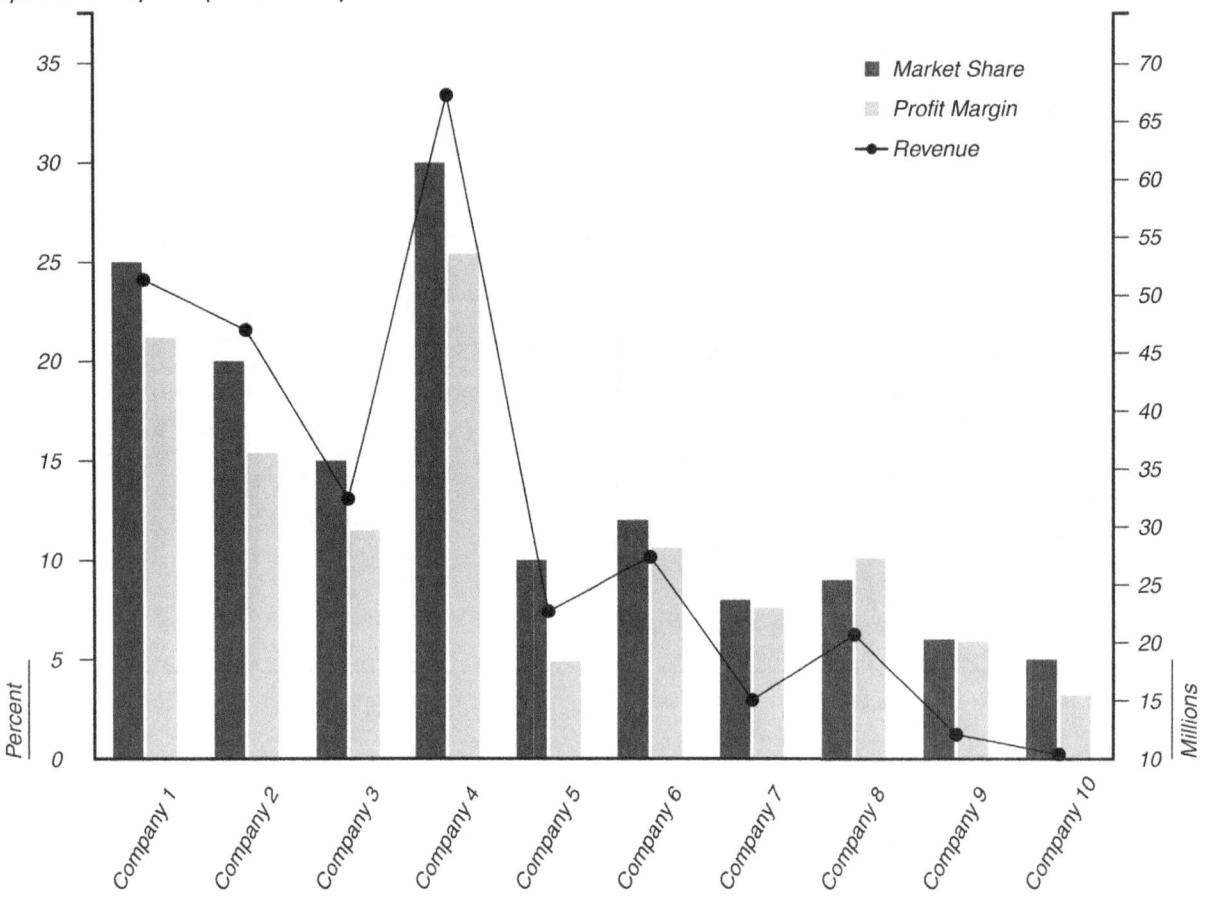

Based on the information in the graph, fill in the blanks:

The difference in market share between the company with the highest revenue and the company with the lowest revenue is _____.
- a. 19%
- b. 21%
- c. 25%
- d. 29%

The average profit margin of companies 2, 4, and 7 combined is _____.
- a. 14%
- b. 16%
- c. 18%
- d. 20%

9. The following graph shows the temperatures (degrees Fahrenheit) over the course of the week of August 4–10, 2024, in Oklahoma City, Washington, D.C., Chicago, and Los Angeles.

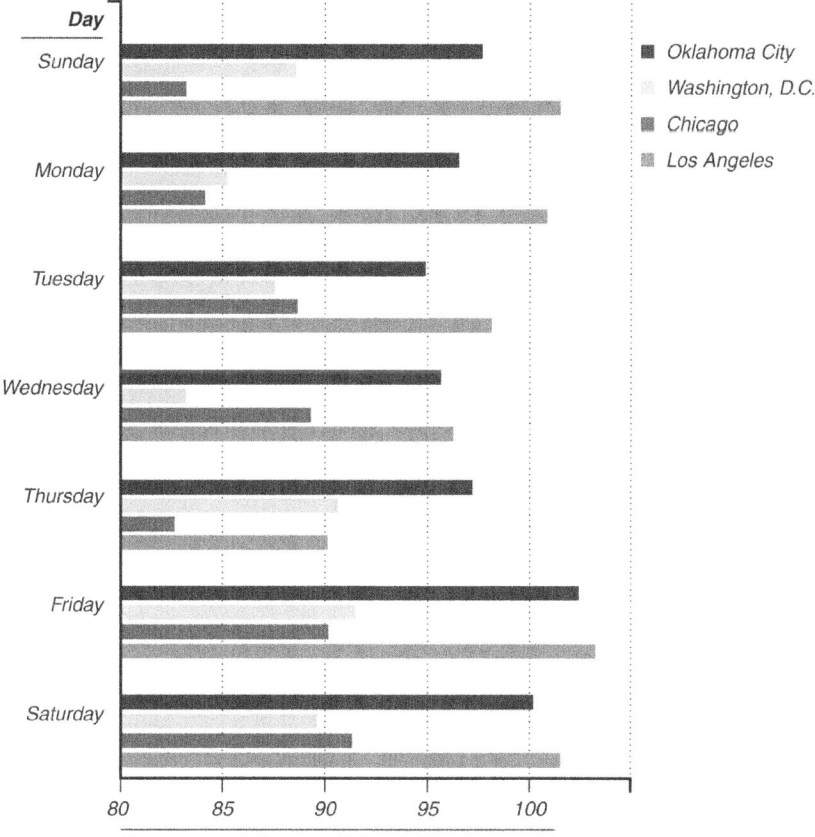

Based on the information in the graph, fill in the blanks:

The temperature difference between Oklahoma City and Chicago was _____ degrees on the day of the week with the largest temperature difference between the two cities.
   a. 5
   b. 15
   c. 20
   d. 25

The average temperature from Tuesday through Thursday in Los Angeles was about _____ degrees higher than the average temperature in Washington, D.C., from Wednesday through Friday.
   a. 2
   b. 6
   c. 10
   d. 15

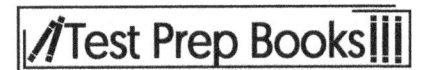

10. A car dealership has kept track of the sales of different types of vehicles over the course of 2023. The following graph shows the total sales for each vehicle type in each quarter, as well as the sales for each month in quarter 1 in more detail.

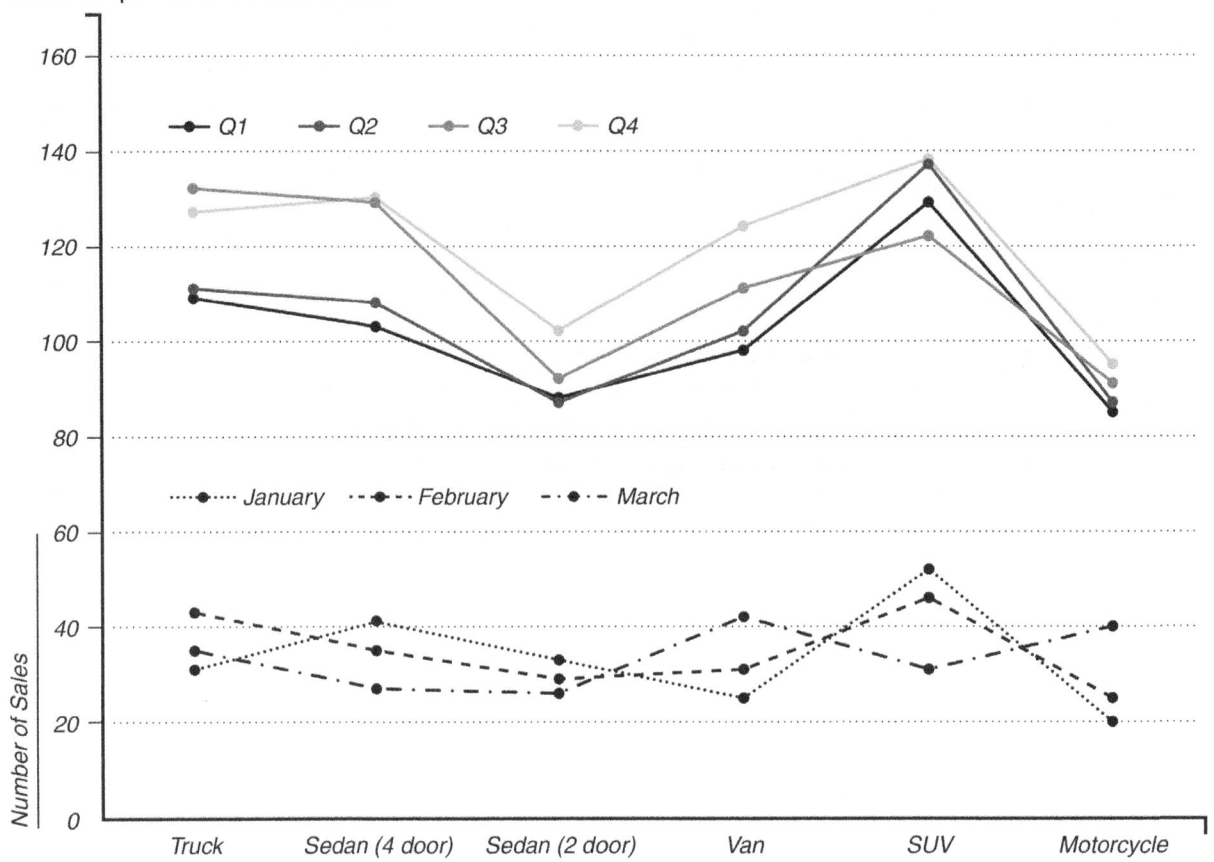

Based on the information in the graph, fill in the blanks:

The percent increase in SUV sales between Q3 and Q4 was _____ than the percent increase in truck sales between Q1 and Q4.
  a. 3.4% more
  b. 2.8% more
  c. 2.8% less
  d. 3.4% less

The total difference in sales between the vehicle that had the highest sales in March and the vehicle that had the lowest sales in Q4 is _____.
  a. 32
  b. 53
  c. 61
  d. 72

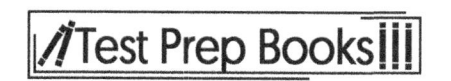

Two-Part Analysis

Read each passage and answer the question at the end of each passage by marking the appropriate answers for each column:

11. A local children's hospital is organizing a series of educational seminars on topics related to different approaches to improving health care among pediatric populations in the community, with a focus on both reducing asthma-related complications during allergy season and disease prevention this upcoming year. Several lectures will be taking place over the course of the first Monday, Tuesday, and Wednesday of February. Seminar 1 needs to take place before Seminar 2 because of a planned transition between related topics, and Seminar 3 must take place sometime on the same day as 1 and 2. Some of the same speakers are involved in Seminars 4 and 5, so they would like to be scheduled on the same day. Seminar 4 cannot be scheduled on Wednesday due to schedule conflicts, and Seminar 5 cannot be scheduled on Tuesday for similar reasons. Finally, Seminar 6 cannot be scheduled on the same day as Seminar 2 because of the way the hospital wants the topics covered. Based on this information, when can Seminar 6 be scheduled, and when can Seminars 4 and 5 both be scheduled?

Make one selection for each column:

Seminar 6	Seminars 4 and 5	
○	○	a. Monday
○	○	b. Tuesday
○	○	c. Monday and Wednesday
○	○	d. Monday, Tuesday, or Wednesday

12. A jewelry boutique sells beaded bracelets, flower earrings, and gemstone necklaces. The store must spend $5 in order to make each beaded bracelet, and they sell for $10 per bracelet. The gemstone necklaces cost $7 each to produce, and they sell for $12 per necklace. The earrings were going to cost $6 to make each pair, and they were going to be sold for $8 per set. Over the course of the last 12 months, the boutique has produced 350 beaded bracelets and sold 300. It produced 275 gemstone necklaces and sold 200. The production of flower earrings was canceled because the materials were found to cause skin irritation, so none were produced or sold. The store incurred $1,000 in fixed costs during this time. What was the total revenue generated in the past year, and what profit did the boutique make last year after taking both fixed costs and production costs into consideration?

Make one selection for each column:

Revenue	Profit	
○	○	a. $725
○	○	b. $850
○	○	c. $2,500
○	○	d. $5,400
○	○	e. $6,200

Table Analysis

13. A family is evaluating their expenses in order to learn to budget better. To do this, they have kept track of their household costs over the past year. The following table lays out their yearly expenses by month and category of expense.

Month	Mortgage	Groceries	Utilities	Other
January	$850.00	$675.24	$450.11	$210.52
February	$850.00	$598.06	$398.39	$410.24
March	$850.00	$475.92	$375.07	$152.11
April	$850.00	$502.44	$362.98	$198.29
May	$850.00	$498.65	$351.22	$258.94
June	$850.00	$520.29	$372.84	$325.81
July	$850.00	$575.33	$390.76	$220.75
August	$850.00	$601.20	$401.55	$110.73
September	$850.00	$599.25	$382.01	$190.74
October	$850.00	$690.11	$390.42	$431.22
November	$850.00	$798.78	$425.84	$323.98
December	$850.00	$725.21	$482.52	$502.21

Check either Yes or No for each of the following statements:

Yes	No	
○	○	The average monthly cost of utilities and other items combined between April and May was at least 15% more than the average monthly cost of groceries between April and May.
○	○	During the months when more was spent on other items than on utilities, more than $600 was spent on groceries.
○	○	The average increase in the percentage spent on utilities between October and December was greater than the percent increase in the amount spent on groceries between September and November.

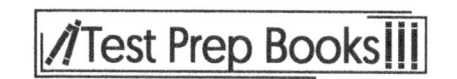

14. A national art museum has recorded the amount of money made (in millions) from adult ticket sales, child ticket sales, gift shop sales, and ticket sales for special events that the museum holds throughout each year. In 2024, adult tickets cost $10.25, and child tickets cost $7.75. Special event pricing varies by event. The following table represents the amount of money made from these categories over the past 10 years (in millions, rounded to the nearest hundredths place):

Year	Adult Ticket Sales	Child Ticket Sales	Gift Shop Sales	Special Event Ticket Sales
2015	$62.42	$25.21	$22.64	$11.89
2016	$74.71	$28.74	$30.25	$12.94
2017	$75.93	$29.39	$33.98	$16.99
2018	$80.11	$32.47	$39.86	$20.32
2019	$81.32	$37.44	$40.93	$21.28
2020	$86.24	$41.21	$45.63	$29.64
2021	$89.59	$43.98	$49.97	$30.11
2022	$94.42	$48.79	$50.23	$34.92
2023	$97.98	$52.84	$51.77	$39.26
2024	$105.24	$57.62	$52.96	$42.64

Choose either Yes or No for each of the following statements:

Yes	No	
○	○	The museum made less off adult ticket sales than child and special event sales between the years of 2015 and 2017.
○	○	More adult tickets were sold between 2020 and 2023 than children's tickets between 2017 and 2020.
○	○	The yearly average increase in sales for children's tickets was greater than $0.12 million more than the average increase in sales for special events.

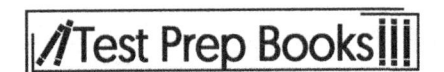

15. A climate research institute measured the average monthly temperatures for Virginia, Oklahoma, New Mexico, and Washington over the course of the past year. The temperatures on average have risen by 2.4 degrees each year in Oklahoma, New Mexico, and Washington over the past 10 years. However, Virginia's average temperature has only risen by 1.9 degrees each year for the past 10 years. The following table represents the average monthly temperatures in degrees Fahrenheit recorded this past year:

Month	Virginia	Oklahoma	New Mexico	Washington
January	35.4	34.1	32.0	30.1
February	34.2	33.8	31.9	31.2
March	40.2	43.7	50.8	39.7
April	58.0	61.2	65.6	55.4
May	61.5	67.3	69.8	59.9
June	75.4	76.8	78.3	64.5
July	76.1	79.4	80.2	67.8
August	77.8	80.9	82.4	71.3
September	70.5	74.3	76.1	68.4
October	63.2	65.4	62.8	55.6
November	52.9	56.1	49.8	47.8
December	45.3	47.2	42.1	36.1

Choose either Yes or No for each of the following statements:

Yes	No	
○	○	The average temperature in New Mexico between June and August 3 years ago was lower than 76 degrees.
○	○	The state with the largest range of average monthly temperatures also had more months with the average temperature in the sixties than any other state.
○	○	The median temperature for Oklahoma is 63.3 degrees.

Data Sufficiency

Decide whether the data given in the statements are sufficient to answer the question.

16. A seafood distribution company has promised to donate x dollars to a wildlife preservation charity for every unit sold in a 90-day period. How much money did the company anticipate donating?

Statement 1: The company anticipated selling 1,500 units during this time.

Statement 2: The company sold 250 more units than it expected to, so the total amount of money it donated was $15,000.

a. Statement (1) ALONE is sufficient, but Statement (2) ALONE is not sufficient.
b. Statement (2) ALONE is sufficient, but Statement (1) ALONE is not sufficient.
c. BOTH statements TOGETHER are sufficient, but NEITHER statement ALONE is sufficient.
d. EACH statement ALONE is sufficient.
e. Statements (1) and (2) TOGETHER are not sufficient.

17. A fitness gear company makes and sells soccer cleats and baseball bats. The total production cost for both of these last year was $300,000. What was the production cost for the cleats?

Statement 1: Bats accounted for 35% of the total production cost.

Statement 2: The production cost for the cleats was $30 per pair, and 6,425 were sold last year.

a. Statement (1) ALONE is sufficient, but Statement (2) ALONE is not sufficient.
b. Statement (2) ALONE is sufficient, but Statement (1) ALONE is not sufficient.
c. BOTH statements TOGETHER are sufficient, but NEITHER statement ALONE is sufficient.
d. EACH statement ALONE is sufficient.
e. Statements (1) and (2) TOGETHER are not sufficient.

18. A farmer installed a new, larger grain silo with a height of 275 feet. What is the volume of the old silo?

Statement 1: The height of the old silo is 225 feet.

Statement 2: The volume of the old silo is 2 million cubic feet smaller than that of the new one.

a. Statement (1) ALONE is sufficient, but Statement (2) ALONE is not sufficient.
b. Statement (2) ALONE is sufficient, but Statement (1) ALONE is not sufficient.
c. BOTH statements TOGETHER are sufficient, but NEITHER statement ALONE is sufficient.
d. EACH statement ALONE is sufficient.
e. Statements (1) and (2) TOGETHER are not sufficient.

19. There are four departments within a company, each of which has its own number of employees. These departments are marketing, HR, sales, and research and development. Sales has twice the employees of HR, and research and development has 10 more than marketing. The total number of employees for all departments at the company is 200. How many employees are there in sales?

Statement 1: The marketing department has 50 employees.

Statement 2: There are 30 people working in the HR department.

a. Statement (1) ALONE is sufficient, but Statement (2) ALONE is not sufficient.
b. Statement (2) ALONE is sufficient, but Statement (1) ALONE is not sufficient.
c. BOTH statements TOGETHER are sufficient, but NEITHER statement ALONE is sufficient.
d. EACH statement ALONE is sufficient.
e. Statements (1) and (2) TOGETHER are not sufficient.

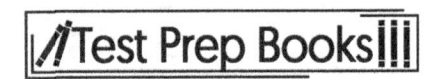

20. Scientists are conducting an experiment in the physics lab at a state college, and they need to find out more about the relationship between variable x and variable y in order to better understand the behavior of the experimental setup. Is variable x greater than variable y?

Statement 1: In their research, the scientists found that the function $f(x, y) = x + y$ is greater than 20.

Statement 2: Additionally, they observed that the function $g(x, y) = x3 - y3$ is a positive number.

a. Statement (1) ALONE is sufficient, but Statement (2) ALONE is not sufficient.
b. Statement (2) ALONE is sufficient, but Statement (1) ALONE is not sufficient.
c. BOTH statements TOGETHER are sufficient, but NEITHER statement ALONE is sufficient.
d. EACH statement ALONE is sufficient.
e. Statements (1) and (2) TOGETHER are not sufficient.

Answer Explanations #1

Quantitative Reasoning

1. D: First, subtract $1,437 from $2,334.50 to find Johnny's monthly savings; this equals $897.50. Then, multiply this amount by 3 to find out how much he will have (in 3 months) before he pays for his vacation; this equals $2,692.50. Finally, subtract the cost of the vacation ($1,750) from this amount to find how much Johnny will have left: $942.50.

2. B: First, calculate the difference between the larger value and the smaller value.

$$378 - 252 = 126$$

This means that there was an increase of 126 customers. Next, find what percent of 252 this would be. To do this set 126 over 252.

$$\frac{126}{252} = .5$$

Now multiply by 100 to turn this into a percent.

$$0.5 \times 100 = 50\%$$

3. C: 40% of y is 24, so $0.4y = 24$. Dividing both sides of the equation by 0.4 results in $y = 60$. Also, it is true that $\frac{60}{120} = 0.5$, so 60 is 50% of 120. Therefore, the answer is 50%.

4. D: The slope from this equation is 50, and it is interpreted as the cost per gigabyte used. Since the g-value represents the number of gigabytes and the equation is set equal to the cost in dollars, the slope relates these two values. For every gigabyte used on the phone, the bill goes up 50 dollars.

5. A: The ratio of fruit to vegetables is 5 to 3, which means that 3 out of every 8 produce items are vegetables. $\frac{3}{8} = 0.375$, and $0.375 \times 120 = 45$. Therefore, 45 of the total 120 produce items are vegetables and $120 - 45 = 75$ are fruit.

6. E: The answer is 64. The first step is to find the value of m. Recall that roots of numbers are the same as fractional exponents:

$$\sqrt[3]{m} = m^{\frac{1}{3}} = 2$$

Both sides of the equation can be raised to the power of 3 to solve for m. Using the power rule, an exponent on an exponent results in multiplying the exponents, canceling out the cube root:

$$\left(m^{\frac{1}{3}}\right)^3 = m^{\frac{1}{3} \times 3} = m = 2^3$$

$$m = 8$$

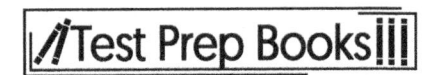

Using the value of m, solve the second equation for n:

$$m = 8 = \sqrt{n}$$

$$n = 8^2$$

$$n = 64$$

Therefore, the correct answer is Choice E, 64.

7. C: This is a probability based on combinations. The probability of selecting a purple and a blue can be calculated by multiplying the number of ways of drawing a purple by the number of ways of drawing a blue then dividing this product by the total number of ways of drawing two marbles of any color. This is equal to:

$$\frac{C_1^{12} \times C_1^8}{C_2^{30}} = \frac{12 \times 8}{\frac{30 \times 29}{2 \times 1}} = \frac{96}{435} = \frac{32}{145}.$$

8. B: The average of the 5 test scores needs to be greater than or equal to 75. Therefore, we have the following inequality:

$$\frac{73(4) + x}{5} \geq 75.$$

Multiply through by 5 to obtain

$$73(4) + x \geq 375.$$

Multiply 73 by 4 to get 292, and subtract this from each side to find that $x \geq 83$.

9. E: The result of 8.4 shows that the quotient is 8 and the remainder, as a decimal, is 0.4. Because the remainder is 9, we know that 9 divided by the unknown quantity (the divisor) is equal to 0.4. Therefore, $\frac{9}{x} = 0.4$. We know that

$$9 = 0.4x, \text{ or } x = 22.5.$$

10. B: The quantity $xy + x$ is negative because a negative times a positive plus a negative is negative. The quantity $y^x + y$ is positive because a positive raised to a negative power plus a positive is still positive. The quantity $x^y - y$ will not always produce a positive integer because a negative raised to a positive power minus a positive could be negative. Finally, xy^2 is a negative times a positive, which is negative.

11. B: Each day, the magazine salesperson needs to sell at least $20 \times 8 = 160$ subscriptions to make quota. To obtain a bonus, they must sell $1.2(160) = 192$ subscriptions. So far today, they have sold $16 + 14 + 18 + 20 + 16 + 28 = 112$ subscriptions. They must sell $192 - 112 = 80$ subscriptions over the course of 2 hours—an average of 40 subscriptions per hour—to earn a bonus.

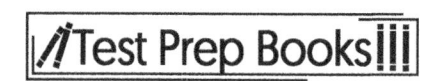

12. C: The easiest way to compute this expression is to convert all of the fractions to equivalent fractions that have the same denominator. The common denominator for the existing denominators—2, 3, 4, 5, 6, and 7—is the least common multiple (LCM) of these values, which is 420. Therefore, we have

$$\left(\frac{210}{420} - \frac{84}{420}\right) + \left(\frac{140}{420} + \frac{84}{420}\right) - \left(\frac{70}{420} + \frac{105}{420}\right) + \left(\frac{140}{420} + \frac{60}{420}\right).$$

Removing the parentheses, we obtain

$$\frac{210}{420} - \frac{84}{420} + \frac{140}{420} + \frac{84}{420} - \frac{70}{420} - \frac{105}{420} + \frac{140}{420} + \frac{60}{420},$$

which simplifies to

$$\frac{375}{420} = \frac{25}{28}.$$

13. E: We are trying to find out how many possible permutations there are of the top 3 out of 5 classrooms. There are 4 options for first place (since one cannot place first this year), 4 options for second place, and 3 options for third place. Therefore, the correct answer is $4 \times 4 \times 3 = 48$ possibilities.

14. B: First, we round each number under the radical to obtain

$$\sqrt{\frac{90(2{,}600)}{16^2}}.$$

This expression is equal to

$$\sqrt{\frac{90(2{,}600)}{256}}.$$

256 can be estimated as 260, which can be divided into the 2,600 in the numerator to obtain

$$\sqrt{90(10)} = \sqrt{900} = 30.$$

The original expression is approximately equal to 30.

15. C: Let y be equal to the capacity of the tank. It is true that

$$\frac{1}{4}y + x = \frac{7}{8}y.$$

Therefore,

$$x = \frac{7}{8}y - \frac{1}{4}y = \frac{5}{8}y.$$

Solve for y to obtain $y = \frac{8}{5}x$.

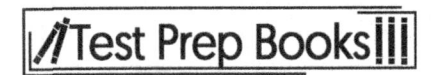

16. C: Possible values of $\frac{x}{4}$ are $2^2, 3^2, 5^2, 7^2, 11^2, 13^2, \ldots$ Therefore, we have that the possible values of x are

$$4 \times 2^2 = 16,$$

$$4 \times 3^2 = 36,$$

$$4 \times 5^2 = 100,$$

$$4 \times 7^2 = 196,$$

and

$$4 \times 11^2 = 484.$$

There are four such x values that fall within the desired range.

17. A: Let x be equal to the total number of agents. It is true that $0.7x$ is equal to the number of full-time agents and $0.3x$ is equal to the number of part-time agents. We have

$$0.3x + 560 = 0.7x.$$

Therefore,

$$560 = 0.4x.$$

Divide both sides by 0.4 to obtain $x = 1400$.

18. B: The arithmetic mean is 7.2, and the standard deviation is 3.15. First, calculate 3 standard deviations by multiplying 3 by 3.15 to obtain 9.45. In order to lie more than 3 standard deviations away from the mean, a number would either need to be less than

$$7.2 - 9.45 = -2.25$$

or greater than

$$7.2 + 9.45 = 16.65.$$

Therefore, -3 is the only choice lying more than 3 standard deviations away from the mean.

19. C: First, we determine which part of the piecewise-defined function we plug -1 into. We choose the function that lies over the interval $-1 \leq x \leq 1$, which is $-5|x|$. Then, we plug -1 into the function. Therefore,

$$f(-1) = -5|-1| = -5(1) = -5.$$

Answer Explanations #1

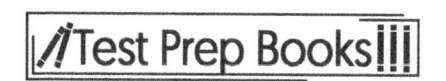

20. E: The probability that Katie will be selected for Monday is $\frac{1}{8}$, and the probability that Joe will be selected for Monday is also $\frac{1}{8}$. Therefore, the probability that both Katie and Joe will be selected for Monday is

$$\frac{1}{8} \times \frac{1}{8} = \frac{1}{64}.$$

The probability that neither of them will present on Monday is

$$1 - \frac{1}{64} = \frac{64}{64} - \frac{1}{64} = \frac{63}{64}.$$

21. A: We use the equation to first solve for x. Rewrite the mixed number as an improper fraction such that $\frac{1}{x} = \frac{13}{3}$. Cross-multiply to obtain

$$3 = 13x$$

or

$$x = \frac{3}{13}.$$

Plug this value into the expression to obtain

$$\left(\frac{2}{\frac{3}{13}+3}\right)^2 = \left(\frac{2}{\frac{3}{13}+\frac{39}{13}}\right)^2 = \left(\frac{2}{\frac{42}{13}}\right)^2 = \frac{4}{\frac{1764}{169}} = 4 \times \frac{169}{1764} = \frac{676}{1764} = \frac{169}{441}.$$

Verbal Reasoning

Reading Comprehension

1. A: Choice A is the correct answer because it accurately describes the primary purpose of the passage. The passage describes the step-by-step process of cellular respiration and explains why each step is important in this process. Choice B is incorrect because the byproducts are only mentioned in the last paragraph to explain what the cells do with the excess byproducts. Choice C is incorrect because specific organisms are never mentioned. Choice D is incorrect because the passage does not describe the process as being inefficient.

2. C: Choice C is the correct answer because both processes create carbon dioxide as a byproduct. This is seen in the last sentence of the second paragraph, which states that carbon dioxide is a byproduct created by the conversion of pyruvate to acetyl-CoA, and in the last sentence of the third paragraph, which states that carbon dioxide is a byproduct of the citric acid cycle. Choices A, B, and D are incorrect because none of those are byproducts of both processes.

3. B: Choice B is the correct answer because during the process of glycolysis a glucose molecule is broken down into two molecules of pyruvate. This information can be found in the second paragraph. Choice A is incorrect because the byproducts of the cellular respiration process are expelled in the later stages. Choice C is incorrect because the electron transport chain and proton gradient occur in the final stage of cellular respiration whereas glycolysis takes place at the beginning. Choice D is incorrect because acetyl-CoA is broken down during the citric acid cycle.

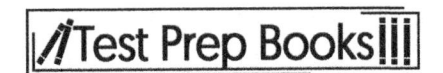

4. D: Choice D is the correct answer because both the water reservoir on one side of a dam and the relatively high proton concentration on one side of the mitochondrial membrane in a proton gradient are sources of potential energy that is then harnessed by turbines and ATP synthase, respectively, to generate usable energy stores.

5. B: Choice B is the correct answer because the passage explains how industries relied on manual labor, animals, and water-powered mills before the steam engine's creation. Choice A is incorrect because traveling long distances was not common before steam-powered transportation. Choice C is incorrect because prior to ships using steam engines, travel and global trade were not extensive since traveling and transporting goods was inefficient. Choice D is incorrect because there is no mention of factories needing to be close to mountains for resources. Rather, the passage suggests that the constraints imposed by the energy sources available prior to the invention of the steam engine hindered some factories from being located near the raw materials they relied upon.

6. A: Choice A is the correct answer because the passage mentions that trains and ships powered by steam engines were revolutionary for travel. This led to increased tourism and enhanced the ability to trade globally as the world became more interconnected. Choice B is incorrect because agriculture and logging are not specifically mentioned as being improved by the steam engine, and although they most likely were, shipping and tourism were affected to a greater extent. Choice C is incorrect because telecommunication and banking were not widely relevant at the time of the invention of the steam engine. Choice D is incorrect because textiles and retail are not mentioned in the passage as being affected by the steam engine.

7. D: Choice D is the correct answer because the passage states that the steam engine allowed factories to be built in advantageous locations near markets and raw materials since they no longer needed to be built along a water source. Choice A is incorrect because global trade would still require factories to produce the goods being traded. Choice B is incorrect because workers would still be needed in order to operate the steam engines. Choice C is incorrect because the passage explicitly states that factories no longer needed water sources.

8. D: Choice D is the correct answer because the passage discusses the advantages and disadvantages of solar and geothermal energy while highlighting the differences between the two. Choice A is incorrect because the passage does not focus on the importance of replacing fossil fuels. Choice B is incorrect because the passage does not discuss financial savings. Choice C is incorrect because the passage does not argue for one energy source over the other.

9. C: Choice C is the correct answer because the passage mentions geographical requirements for geothermal energy plants in order to highlight a major limitation of geothermal energy use—it cannot be implemented on a widespread basis due to its limited geographical availability. Choice A is incorrect because the passage does not mention the cost of implementing geothermal electricity generation. Choice B is incorrect because the passage mentions the location limitation objectively and does not attempt to make an argument against the use of geothermal energy. Choice D is incorrect because the author is not presenting one energy option as being superior to the other but is simply presenting facts about each option.

Answer Explanations #1

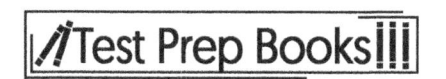

10. C: Choice *C* is the correct answer because the passage indicates that geothermal power plants must be located near volcanic or tectonic activity. The rain is irrelevant since geothermal energy is not dependent on weather like solar energy is. Choices *A*, *B*, and *D* are incorrect because they do not include volcanic or tectonic activity, which are necessary for extracting geothermal energy to produce electricity. Choices *A* and *B* would most likely be well suited for solar energy harnessing.

11. B: Choice *B* is the correct answer because the passage mentions non-essential and luxury goods to show how price changes affect demand differently depending on the type of product being sold. It emphasizes the way in which consumer behavior differs depending on whether or not they consider the product to be a necessity. Choice *A* is incorrect because the passage is not arguing about the importance of luxury goods for the economy. Choice *C* is incorrect because the author is not attempting to persuade the audience to abstain from purchasing luxury goods; they are simply educating readers about price demand elasticity. Choice *D* is incorrect because although socioeconomic standing may be related to the topic of luxury good price elasticity, it is not explicitly discussed within the text.

12. C: Choice *C* is the correct answer because it describes a situation in which a slight increase in the price of a luxury product leads to a significant decrease in the demand for that product. A *significant* decrease in demand in response to a *slight* increase in price fits the definition of elastic demand since the change in demand is disproportionately large compared to the change in price (elasticity greater than 1). Choice *A* is incorrect because the demand for the common medication stays the same, therefore it is not elastic. Choice *B* is incorrect because there is only a small increase in demand. Choice *D* is incorrect because gasoline is typically considered an essential good, and an increase in demand despite a price increase would indicate inelastic demand, not elastic demand.

13. B: Choice *B* is the correct answer because the passage explains that businesses consider price elasticity of demand in order to maximize profits by determining how price changes might affect consumer behavior. This is discussed in the last paragraph of the passage. Choice *A* is incorrect because it is policymakers, not businesses, who protect consumers. Choice *C* is incorrect because the price elasticity of demand does not necessarily influence the cost of production for goods. It is focused on the relationship between the price of the goods and their demand. Choice *D* is incorrect because brand loyalty is not discussed in the passage in relation to price elasticity.

Critical Reasoning

14. A: Choice *A* is very strong since it provides an alternate explanation for the high valuation other than Julia. If the Company released an extremely popular application, then the application is the real reason for the 10 million dollar valuation. Furthermore, this answer choice explicitly states that the application was released before Julia's hiring. Keep this choice for now.

Choice *B* is irrelevant. Whether investors are properly evaluating the Company's price does not affect Julia's role in that valuation. Eliminate this choice.

Choice *C* strengthens the argument. If Julia is an expert in her field, then her skills could have been the reason for the valuation. Investors could have factored in Julia's expertise in their valuation. It definitely does not weaken the argument. Eliminate this choice.

Choice *D* is another strong answer choice. If Julia only worked at Michael Scott Paperless Company for two weeks, then it is less likely that she's the reason for the 10 million dollar valuation. However, if she's a renowned expert or extreme talent, then her hiring alone could have affected the valuation. This answer choice is less strong than Choice A, which provides a clear alternative explanation for the sudden increase in valuation. Since Choice A is stronger, eliminate Choice D.

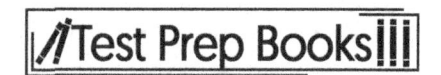

Choice E strengthens the argument. If Julia completed two important projects during her first month, then she could very well be the reason for the valuation. It definitely does not weaken the argument; eliminate Choice E as well.

Therefore, Choice A is the correct answer.

15. C: Choice A does not identify a flaw in the advertisement's reasoning. The advertisement connects smoking with fatal disease. At no point does the advertisement confuse the cause and effect. Eliminate this choice.

Choice B is incorrect. The advertisement does not make any overly broad generalizations. Eliminate this choice.

Choice C correctly identifies the argument's flaw. The argument analogizes secondhand smoke with a gas chamber without offering any evidence concerning secondhand smoke's health risk. The advertisement is clearly relying on hyperbole. The advertisement's argument properly justifies smoking with adverse health effects, but it does not do the same for secondhand smoke. This is most likely the correct answer.

Choice D is incorrect. Nothing in the argument states that there's real dispute over smoking's effect on health. Eliminate this choice.

Choice E is not present in the argument. Eliminate this choice.

16. D: Choice D is the correct answer because studies showing that Blue Zone natives have genetic traits protecting them against disease would weaken the argument that the extended life expectancies are due solely to lifestyle factors. This would be compelling evidence that genetics also contribute to Blue Zone residents' longer-than-average lifespans. Choice A is incorrect because the type of employment of Blue Zone residents versus those living outside of Blue Zones is not information that weakens the argument. Choices B and C are incorrect because there are elements other than diet included in the argument that Blue Zone residents' extended life expectancies are attributable to lifestyle factors rather than to genetics. Choice E is incorrect because it strengthens the original argument. If young individuals can achieve a similar lifespan as native residents, it would suggest that there are factors other than genetics at play. This supports the author's argument that factors such as diet, exercise, and community are more significant than genetics.

17. B: Choice B is the correct answer because it strengthens the argument by providing data that suggests that outdoor classrooms may have a positive impact on students' educational success as demonstrated by those students achieving higher test scores than students whose schools do not utilize outdoor classrooms. Choice A is incorrect because outdoor classrooms being more beneficial in certain months does not strengthen the argument, especially since most schools are closed during the summer months. Choice C is incorrect because the topic at hand is about outdoor classrooms that exist within a school's campus. While field trips may take place outdoors, they are not directly related to the topic of outdoor classrooms. Therefore, mentioning their benefits does not strengthen the argument. Choice D is incorrect because the research mentioned does not address whether outdoor classrooms have a positive effect on educational performance. Choice E is incorrect because while the benefits derived are

Answer Explanations #1

relevant and are related to student activities in an outdoor school setting, they are the result of outdoor extracurricular school activities rather than outdoor classrooms.

18. D: Choice *D* is the correct answer because it is central to the counterclaim. If pesticides were the only cause for the decline of bee populations, then banning them would stabilize bee populations. However, if bee populations continue to decline after pesticides have been banned, that means that there are other factors at play. Choice *A* is incorrect because the effects of certain types of pesticides are not central to the counterclaim, which depends on other factors affecting bee populations. Choice *B* is incorrect because the difficulty of identifying and measuring the impact of other factors such as climate change does not change their significance in the decline of bee populations. This does not affect the comparison of pesticides with other factors. Choice *C* is incorrect because the effect of pesticides and factors such as habitat loss on bee populations can be measured and compared regardless of regulations. The relative regulation of the factors is not relevant to the counterclaim. Choice *E* is incorrect because based on the counterclaim, habitat loss is an equally significant contributor to bee population decline. Therefore, habitat conservation should improve bee populations even when pesticides are also a factor.

19. C: Choice *C* is the correct answer because it weakens the original argument by showing that exercising 30 minutes per day may not be the best way to improve memory. If meditating is just as effective, exercise is simply one of multiple equally effective methods of improving memory. Choice *A* is incorrect because the topic of the argument is improving memory performance, not overall health; therefore, this statement neither strengthens nor weakens the argument. Choice *B* is incorrect because although it appears to point to a negative aspect of performing highly on memory tests, it does not weaken the author's specific argument. Choice *D* is incorrect because it strengthens the author's argument by indicating that 30 minutes of exercise per day is correlated with greater improvements in individuals' performance on memory tests than 2 hours of exercise once per week. Choice *E* is incorrect because the passage does not argue for the longevity of the memory improvement, simply that consistent, daily exercise is the best way to achieve it. This answer choice does not weaken that claim since the reduction in memory improvements results from inconsistency in the exercise routine.

20. B: Choice *B* is the correct answer because it proves that a dedicated employee can do the same job as the software, but with significantly fewer errors. This supports the supervisor's suggestion that having a dedicated employee would be better for the company. Choice *A* is incorrect because although software may take adjustment, so would a new employee. Therefore, this does not necessarily strengthen the supervisor's argument. Choice *C* is incorrect because it emphasizes the efficiency of automation software, and increased efficiency is what the company hopes to attain by implementing the software. Employee satisfaction may not be as high of a priority to the company. Choice *D* is incorrect because the financial benefits of implementing project management software would support their implementation rather than the argument for having a dedicated employee handle the tasks. Choice *E* is incorrect because it does not support the supervisor's argument that a dedicated employee should be used instead of software. This answer choice suggests that using them together is the best option.

21. D: Choice *D* is the correct answer because the fact that the majority of city residents would be unable to utilize public transportation for their daily commute indicates that there would still be traffic problems after expanding the public transportation system. Choice *A* is incorrect because it supports the city planners' argument by suggesting that traffic congestion will continue to increase if the public transportation system is not expanded. Choice *B* is incorrect because the positive correlation between extensive public transportation systems and economic growth does not present an argument against the conclusion that expanding the public transportation system would resolve all of the city's traffic problems. Choice C is incorrect because the concern about tax increases does not affect the effectiveness of the public transportation system. Choice E is incorrect because even though it points out a negative consequence of expanding a public transportation system, it does not directly relate to the argument about the public transportation system solving traffic congestion.

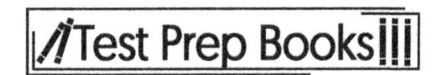

22. D: Choice D is correct because it highlights a specific counterargument to the assertion that library programs are an easy way to improve literacy skills in young children. Difficulty accessing libraries, due to a lack of transportation or time, presents a barrier that would likely make library-run literacy programs more difficult for these families than other literacy interventions. Choice A is incorrect because the success of after-school programs does not weaken or negate the convenience of library programs. Choice B is incorrect because libraries' contribution to improved literacy rates through providing free books for children before they enter school strengthens, rather than weakens, the argument that library-run programs are the easiest way to improve literacy rates for children. Choice C is incorrect because funding challenges do not affect the convenience of library programs for some families and communities. Choice E is incorrect because the effectiveness of one-on-one tutoring programs neither adds to nor detracts from the ease of access and effectiveness of library-run programs, which is what the passage's argument is about.

23. D: Choice D is the correct answer because it provides a compelling argument for why other options should not be abolished in case digital payment methods cease to work. Physical payment methods such as cash are an important backup for when technology fails. Choice A is incorrect because while it indicates that consumers prefer cash, it does not argue against the claim that digital payment is more secure and convenient. Choice B is incorrect because consumer wariness about digital payment options does not make it less convenient or secure. Choice C is incorrect because it strengthens the argument by providing statistical data regarding the improved efficiency of digital payment options. Choice E is incorrect because it supports Alex's point regarding the security of digital payment systems.

Data Insights

Multi-Source Reasoning

1. C: To begin, find the total increase in the number of tourists between 2019 and 2023 by subtracting 2.1 (million) from 4.8 (million) to get 2.7 (million) tourists. Next, calculate the number of years that passed during that time by subtracting 2019 from 2023 to get 4 years. Finally, divide 2.7 by 4 to get an average annual increase of 0.675 (million) tourists in San Francisco between 2019 and 2023.

2. Yes, No, No: For the first statement, refer to Tab 1. Begin by calculating 20% of the total number of tourists in 2020 by multiplying 0.2 by 2.6 (million) to get 0.52 (million). Next, subtract 0.52 (million) from the total of 2.6 (million) to calculate the threshold of 2.08 (million). Finally compare this threshold to the number of tourists in 2017, 1.4 (million). Since 1.4 (million) is less than 2.08 (million), the number of tourists in 2017 was at least 20% less than the number of tourists in 2020.

For the second statement, begin by calculating the total cost of improvements to infrastructure from 2016 to 2019. Tab 3 shows that infrastructure accounts for 35% of costs each year; apply this to the information from Tab 1 for the calculations. For 2016, $32,100 × 0.35 = $11,235; for 2017, $27,025 × 0.35 = $9,458.75; for 2018, $31,750 × 0.35 = $11,112.50; for 2019, $36,075 × 0.35 = $12,626.25. Add

Answer Explanations #1

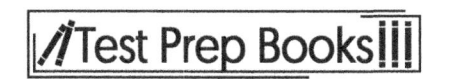

these numbers together to get the total amount spent on infrastructure during that time: $11,235 + $9,458.75 + $11,112.50 + $12,626.25 = $44,432.50. Next, calculate the average cost of all improvements between 2020 and 2022 by adding together the cost of improvements for each of those years and dividing that by the number of years: $45,000 + $44,250 + $48,275 = $137,525 ÷ 3 years = $45,841.67. Since the amount spent on infrastructure between 2016 and 2019 ($44,432.50) is less than the average spent on all improvements from 2020 through 2022 ($45,841.67), the correct answer is *No*.

For the third statement, refer to Tab 3. Public transportation accounted for 25% of costs, infrastructure accounted for 35%, and hotels accounted for 20%. 25% + 35% + 20% = 80%. Since 80% is less than 85%, the answer is *No*.

3. D: For the first statement, add together the costs for each year found in Tab 1 to get a total of $371,725. Divide that number by 10 (the total number of years) to get an average cost of $37,172.50. Since this is greater than $36,500, the first statement is true.

For the second statement, look to Tab 3 to see that 15% of costs each year went towards improving city attractions. Then, find in Tab 1 that the total cost of improvements in 2015 was $30,500. Multiply 0.15 by $30,500 to find that the city spent $4,575 on attractions in 2015, which means that this statement is accurate.

For statement number three, look to the table in Tab 2 and arrange the number of tourists from smallest to greatest: 0.85, 1.0, 1.2, 1.4, 1.7, 2.1, 2.6, 3.5, 4.2, and 4.8. Take the two middle numbers and average them: (1.7 + 2.1) ÷ 2 = 1.9, which means that the third statement is correct.

For the fourth statement, begin by using the information in Tab 2 to calculate the total increase in tourists between 2014 and 2021: 3.5 (million) − 0.85 (million) = 2.65 (million). Next, calculate the number of years that passed during that time: 2021 − 2014 = 7 years. Finally, divide 2.65 (million) by 7 to get the average annual increase in tourists for that time period: 0.38 (million). This means that the fourth statement is not correct.

For the final statement, begin by finding the total amount spent over the past ten years based on the information in Tab 1. This should give you $371,725. Refer to percentages in Tab 3 to calculate the total amount spent on public transportation and hotels. Public transportation: $371,725 x 0.25 = $92,931.25. Hotels: $371,725 x 0.2 = $74,345. Finally, subtract $74,345 from $92,931.25 to find that a total of $18,586.25 more was spent on public transportation than hotels over the past ten years, which means this statement is correct.

4. A: Begin to solve this by calculating the annual population growth rate from 2023 to 2024 using the populations from those years: growth rate = ([920,024 − 911,907] ÷ 911,907) × 100 = 0.89%. Next, use the formula for compound growth rate to calculate the anticipated population for 2027. P_{2027} = 920,024 × $(1 + 0.0089)^3$ = 944,807. Then, calculate the percentage of people who will have a master's degree in 2027. If it is supposed to increase by 2% each year and the percentage in 2024 is 30%, it will be 36% in 2027. This means 944,807 × 0.36 = 340,131 people will have a master's degree in 2027.

5. No, Yes, Yes: For the first statement, begin by calculating the population increase from 2016 to 2017. 855,091 − 847,008 = 8,083. Then, calculate the average annual increase in the number of people with a master's degree between 2015 and 2021. The number of people with a master's degree in 2015 was 0.30 × 832,194 = 249,658 people. The number of people with a master's degree in 2021 was 0.30 × 893,465 = 268,040 people. Calculate the difference by subtracting the number in 2015 from the number in 2021. 268,040 − 249,658 = 18,382. Use the difference to calculate the average annual increase. 18,382 ÷ 6 = 3,064. Since the average annual increase in people with a master's degree between 2015 and 2021 (3,064) is less than the population increase between 2016 and 2017 (8,083), the answer is *No*.

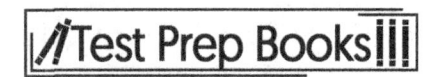

For the second statement, begin by finding the number of people in 2018 who did not own a home. The population in 2018 was 862,034. Find the percentage of non-homeowners by subtracting 64.5% from 100% to get 35.5% Get the number of people who did not own homes in 2018 by multiplying this percentage by the population: 0.355 × 862,034 = 306,022. Next, use the populations from 2015 and 2024 to calculate the total population increase during that time: 920,024 − 832,194 = 87,830. Because the number of people who did not own homes in 2018 (306,022) is more than the population increase between 2015 and 2024 (87,830), the answer to the second statement is *Yes*.

For the third statement, the information in Tabs 1 and 3 indicates that the current percentage of people who own homes is 64.5%, and the city is implementing multiple programs to help incentivize more people to buy homes as well as to help people financially in order to prevent them from losing their homes. Therefore, it is likely that the percentage of people who own homes in the coming years will increase, and the correct answer is *Yes*.

6. C: For the first statement, begin by using the populations from 2020 and 2024 to calculate the percent increase in population during that time: ([920,024 − 882,099] ÷ 882,099) × 100 = 4.3%. Next, use the house prices from 2018 and 2022 to find the percent increase in house prices for that time: ([425,507 − 375,075] ÷ 375,075) × 100 = 13.45%. Since the average percent increase in house prices was greater than the percent increase in population, the first statement is incorrect.

For the second statement, start by using the populations from 2023 and 2024 to calculate the population growth rate during that time: ([920,024 − 911,907] ÷ 911,907) × 100 = 0.89%. Use this, along with the population from 2024, to calculate the projected population for 2025: 920,024 × (1 + 0.0089) = 928,212 people in 2025. If 64.5% of people own homes, 100 − 64.5 = 35.5% of people do not own homes. Multiply the population in 2025 by 35.5% to get the population of non-homeowners in 2025: 928,212 × 0.355 = 329,515, so the second statement is not correct.

For the third statement, there is no data provided showing the numbers of homeowners for each education level. Therefore, this statement is not correct.

For the fourth statement, begin by using the house prices from 2015 and 2020 to calculate the percent increase: ([400,075 − 325,609] ÷ 325,609) × 100 = 22.87%. Then, use the prices from 2020 and 2024 to find the increase in percentage for that time: ([475,504 − 400,075] ÷ 400,075) × 100 = 18.85%. Because the average percent increase in prices for 2015 to 2020 was more than the average percent increase for 2020 to 2024, the fourth statement is not correct.

For the fifth statement, start by looking at Tab 2 to find that the average price of a house in 2024 is $475,504. Next, perform the following calculation to find 1% of this price: .01 × 475,504 = 4,755.04. Tab 2 states that the average cost of a rental in 2024 is $2,400, which is less than $4,755.04. Therefore, this statement is correct.

Answer Explanations #1

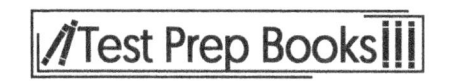

Graphics Interpretation

7. B, C: For the first sentence, find the percent increase by calculating ([Q3 − Q1] ÷ Q1) × 100. Based on the information from the graph, percent increase = ([500 − 425] ÷ 425) × 100 = 17.6%. Therefore, the correct answer is Choice *B*.

For the second sentence, begin by looking at the graph to see the values of each of the factories in Q1 2021. Factory 1: 400, Factory 2: 420, Factory 3: 520, and Factory 4: 300. Then look to see when each one reached 100 more than its starting amount. Factory 1 reached at least 500 in Q1 2022, Factory 2 reached at least 520 in Q4 2021, Factory 3 reached at least 620 in Q2 2022, and Factory 4 reached at least 400 in Q4 2021. Therefore, Factory 3 was the last to reach 100 more than its production in Q1 2021, and Choice *C* is correct.

8. C, B: Begin answering for the first sentence by identifying which companies have the highest and lowest revenues. Highest = Company 4. Lowest = Company 10. Next, identify their market shares. Company 4: 30%. Company 10: 5%. Finally, subtract to find the difference: 30% − 5% = 25%, so the correct answer is Choice *C*.

For the second sentence, start by identifying the profit margins of the appropriate companies. Company 2: 15%, Company 4: 25%, and Company 7: 8%. Then, average these together: (15 + 25 + 8) ÷ 3 = 16%, so Choice *B* is the correct answer.

9. B, B: For the first sentence, begin by finding the approximate difference in temperature between Oklahoma and Chicago for each day of the week, given the data in the graph. Sunday: 98 − 83 = 15. Monday: 96 − 84 = 12. Tuesday: 95 − 89 = 6. Wednesday: 96 − 89 = 7. Thursday: 97 − 83 = 14. Friday: 102 − 90 = 12. Saturday: 100 − 91 = 9. The highest temperature difference of the week was a difference of around 15 degrees, so Choice *B* is correct.

For the second sentence, begin by finding the approximate temperatures in Los Angeles on the appropriate days: Tuesday: 98, Wednesday: 96, and Thursday: 90. Then, find the average of these temperatures: (98 + 96 + 90) ÷ 3 = 95 degrees. Next, do the same for Washington, D.C., for the necessary days: Wednesday: 83, Thursday: 91, and Friday: 92. Find the average: (83 + 91 + 92) ÷ 3 = 88.7 degrees. Finally, find the temperature difference by subtracting the average temperature in Washington, D.C., from the average temperature in Los Angeles: 95 − 88.7 = 6.3, so the correct answer is Choice *B*.

10. D, B: Use the formula for percent increase to make the calculations for the first sentence. Percent increase = ([New Value − Old Value] ÷ Old Value) × 100. For the SUVs between Q3 and Q4, ([138 − 122] ÷ 122) × 100 = 13.11%. For the trucks between Q1 and Q4, ([127 − 109] ÷ 109) × 100 = 16.51%. Next, find the difference between the percentages: 16.51% (trucks) − 13.11 (SUVs) = 3.4% less, so Choice *D* is the correct answer.

Begin answering for the second sentence by finding which vehicle in Q4 had the highest sales in March (vans, with 42 sold) and which vehicle had the lowest sales in October (motorcycles, with 95 sold). Then subtract to find the difference: 95 − 42 = 53, so the correct answer is Choice *B*.

Test Prep Books

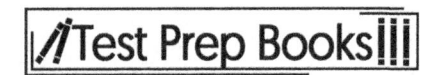

Answer Explanations #1

Two-Part Analysis

11. Seminar 6 is D: Seminar 6 cannot be scheduled on the same day as Seminar 2, and Seminars 1, 2, and 3 must be on the same day. However, since Seminar 6 does not have any other constraints, it can be scheduled for Monday, Tuesday, or Wednesday.

Seminars 4 and 5 is A: Seminars 4 and 5 must take place on the same day. Seminar 5 cannot be on Tuesday, and Seminar 4 cannot be scheduled on Wednesday. Therefore, they must be scheduled on Monday.

12. Revenue is D: The total revenue from bracelets can be calculated by taking $10 per bracelet multiplied by 300 bracelets sold to get $3,000 in revenue from the bracelets. Then multiply $12 per necklace by 200 necklaces sold to get $2,400. Add $3,000 to $2,400 to get a total revenue of $5,400. The earrings can be disregarded because they never went to production.

Profit is A: In order to calculate the profit, first calculate the production costs. Multiply 350 by $5 to get $1,750 in production costs for the bracelets. Multiply $7 by 275 to get $1,925 in production costs for the necklaces. The earrings can be disregarded since production was canceled. Add $1,750 to $1,925 to get a total production cost of $3,675. Take the total revenue of $5,400 and subtract the total production cost of $3,675 and the fixed cost of $1,000 to get a profit of $725.

Table Analysis

13. Yes, No, No: For the first statement, begin by calculating the amount spent on utilities and other items combined in April and May. April: 362.98 + 198.29 = $561.27. May: 351.22 + 258.94 = $610.16. Then, average these together: (561.27 + 610.16) ÷ 2 = $585.72. Next, calculate the average cost of groceries between April ($502.44) and May ($498.65): (502.44 + 498.65) ÷ 2 = $500.55. To see if the cost of utilities and other items was at least 15% more than groceries, use the following calculation: 500.55 × (1 + 0.15) = 575.63. Since 585.72 is greater than 575.63, the correct answer is *Yes*.

For the second statement, start by noting which months more money was spent on other items than on groceries, and note how much was spent on groceries for each of those months. February: $598.06, October: $690.11, and December: $725.21. Since less than $600 was spent on groceries in February, the statement is not accurate.

For the third statement, begin by finding the percent increase in utilities between October and December using the utility prices for those months: ([482.52 − 390.42] ÷ 390.42) × 100 = 23.59%. Proceed by calculating the percent increase in grocery expenses between September and November using the grocery costs for those months: ([798.78 − 599.25] ÷ 599.25) × 100 = 33.3%. Since 23.59% is less than 33.3%, the answer to the third statement is *No*.

14. No, Yes, Yes: Begin to address the first statement by finding the adult ticket sales for 2015 through 2017. 2015: $62.42 million, 2016: $74.71 million, 2017: $75.93 million. Add these together to get a total of $213.06 million for adult ticket sales between 2015 and 2017. Next, find the amounts for child ticket sales and special event sales for the same years. For child tickets, 2015: $25.21 million, 2016: $28.74 million, 2017: $29.39 million. Add these together to get a total of $83.34 million. For special event ticket sales, 2015: $11.89 million, 2016: $12.94 million, 2017: $16.99 million. Add these together to get $41.82 million. Finally, add together to totals for the child and special event ticket sales and compare this

Answer Explanations #1

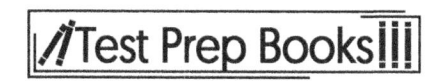

number to the total made from adult ticket sales. $41.82 million + $83.34 million = $125.16 million. Because this is less than $213.06 million, the correct answer to this statement is *No*.

For the second statement, list the amounts made off adult ticket sales each year from 2020 through 2023 and add them together to get the total. 2020: $86.24 million, 2021: $89.59 million, 2022: $94.42 million, 2023: $97.98 million. Total: $368.23 million. Then do the same for child ticket sales from 2017 through 2020. 2017: $29.39 million, 2018: $32.47 million, 2019: $37.44 million, 2020: $41.21 million. Total: $140.51 million. Finally, divide the totals by the adult and children's ticket prices, respectively: $368.23 million ÷ $10.25 = 36 million tickets, $140.51 million ÷ $7.75 = 18 million tickets. Since 36 million is more than 18 million, the correct answer is *Yes*.

Begin solving the third statement by calculating the average annual increase in children's tickets. Find the total increase and divide it by the number of years: $57.62 million − $25.21 million = $32.41 million ÷ 9 years = an average yearly increase of $3.60 million. Next, do the same for special event ticket sales: $42.64 million − $11.89 million = $30.75 million ÷ 9 years = an average yearly increase of $3.42 million. Finally, calculate the difference: $3.60 million − $3.42 million = $0.18 million. Since this number is greater than $0.12 million, this statement is accurate.

15. Yes, No, Yes: For the first statement, average together the average temperatures in New Mexico for June, July, and August: (78.3 + 80.2 + 82.4) ÷ 3 = 80.3 degrees. Next, account for the fact that the temperature has gone up by 2.4 degrees each year to find what the average temperature was during that time 3 years ago: 80.3 − (2.4 × 3) = 73.1 degrees, which is less than 76 degrees. This means that the answer to this statement is *Yes*.

For the second statement, subtract the lowest temperature from the highest temperature in each state to find the range: Virginia (43.6), Oklahoma (47.1), New Mexico (50.5), and Washington (41.2). Then count the number of months in which the temperatures averaged in the sixties for each state: Virginia (2), Oklahoma (3), New Mexico (3), and Washington (3). The state with the largest range is New Mexico, but it has the same number of months with temperatures in the sixties as Oklahoma and Washington. This means that the answer to this statement is *No*.

For the third statement, list the temperatures for Oklahoma in ascending order, then find the middle value or values. Since there are 12 numbers, average the middle 2 values to find the median: (61.2 + 65.4) ÷ 2 = 63.3 degrees, so this statement is accurate.

Data Sufficiency

16. C: From the question, the goal is to solve for x in order to figure out how much money the company anticipated donating. Statement 1 indicates that 1,500 units were expected to be sold, so $1,500x$ represents the answer to the original question. However, this is not enough information to solve for x and be able to get the answer. Statement 2 indicates that the company donated a total of $15,000 after selling 250 more units than expected, but this alone would not be enough information to solve for x. Combining the information from both statements, $1,500x = 15,000 − 250x$. From there, solve for x to get the number of dollars donated per unit and multiply that by 1,500 units to get the total amount that the company anticipated donating.

17. A: The first statement indicates that bats were 35% of the production cost, so the production cost for the cleats can be calculated as follows: 100% − 35% = 65%. 300,000 × 0.65 = $195,000. The second statement provides the number of cleats sold but not the number produced. Therefore, Statement 1 is sufficient, but Statement 2 is not.

18. E: The first statement provides the height of the old silo, but it does not provide the radius needed to calculate the volume. The second statement indicates how much smaller the volume of the old one is compared to the new one but does not provide the volume of the new one to compare. Therefore, Statements 1 and 2 together are not sufficient.

19. D: Statement 1 indicates that marketing has 50 employees. Since research and development has 10 more than that, it has 60 employees. Use this to create the formula: 50 (employees in marketing) + 60 (employees in research and development) + x (employees in HR) + $2x$ (employees in sales) = 200 total employees. From there, solve for x to get 60 employees in the sales department. Statement 2 indicates that 30 people work in HR, and since the problem states that twice as many people work in sales as in HR, this information can be used to calculate that 60 people work in the sales department. Therefore, each statement alone is sufficient.

20. B: Statement 1 provides enough information to know that $x + y > 20$, but it does not provide enough information to find the value of x or y individually, so it is not sufficient. Statement 2 indicates that $x^3 - y^3 > 0$, which means that $x^3 > y^3$ because the cube function is strictly increasing. Therefore, $x > y$, and Statement 2 is sufficient.

Practice Test #2

Quantitative Reasoning

1. A grocery store makes fruit baskets to sell for gifts. They can include apples, oranges, peaches, pears, and plums. They sell packages offering either 16 pieces of the same fruit or 16 pieces consisting of 4 pieces of each of 4 different types of fruit. Each basket can have a ribbon or a balloon. How many different types of fruit baskets are possible?
    a. 10
    b. 15
    c. 20
    d. 120
    e. 42

2. Let a, b, and c be integers such that $a > b > c > 2$. Which of the following has the largest value?
    a. $a(b + c)$
    b. $b(a + c)$
    c. $2(a + b)$
    d. $a(2 + c)$
    e. $c(2 + a)$

3. The quotient when a number is divided by $\frac{5}{6}$ is equal to $\frac{4}{3}$ of $\frac{33}{8}$. What is that number?
    a. $\frac{55}{12}$
    b. $\frac{33}{5}$
    c. $\frac{12}{55}$
    d. $\frac{11}{6}$
    e. $\frac{11}{5}$

4. There exists a sequence of 4 numbers in which each number after the first number is half the previous number squared. The first number is 28. How many of the numbers are multiples of 7?
    a. 1
    b. 2
    c. 3
    d. 4
    e. 5

5. Which of the following numbers is 146 more than $\frac{5}{6}$ of itself?
    a. 926
    b. 25
    c. 175
    d. 881
    e. 876

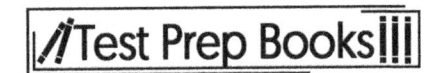

6. Let x be equal to the average of the first 8 positive multiples of 6 and X be equal to the median of the first 8 positive multiples of 6. Compute the quantity $X - x$.
   a. 9
   b. 6
   c. 0
   d. -6
   e. 3

7. A collection of 25 quarters and dimes is in a jar. The total of these coins adds up to $5.80. How many dimes are in the jar?
   a. 22
   b. 8
   c. 25
   d. 6
   e. 3

8. Consider the following inequality: $x^2 - 8 < 0$. Which of the following intervals covers all possible values of x?
   a. $0 < x < 2\sqrt{2}$
   b. $-2\sqrt{2} < x < 0$
   c. $-2\sqrt{2} < x < 2\sqrt{2}$
   d. $-8 < x < 8$
   e. $-8 < x < 0$

9. Let x be an odd number. The median of x consecutive integers is equal to 160. What is the smallest value of these integers?
   a. $\frac{160-x}{2}$
   b. $160 + \frac{x-1}{2}$
   c. $160 - \frac{x}{2}$
   d. $160 - \frac{x-1}{2}$
   e. $\frac{160x}{2}$

10. 20% of a grocery store's inventory consists of produce, and 5% of their produce consists of apples. If a randomly selected piece of inventory is chosen, what is the probability that it will be an apple?
    a. 10%
    b. 1%
    c. 25%
    d. 15%
    e. .01%

11. Krista, a gym teacher, has an equal number of basketballs, baseballs, and soccer balls in storage. She wants to arrange the basketballs into groups of 12, the baseballs into groups of 8, and the soccer balls into groups of 7. What is the least amount of each type of ball Krista has to have to make these groups possible without any balls left over?
   a. 683
   b. 710
   c. 27
   d. 84
   e. 168

12. Solve for a in the following equation:

$$5^{(a-16+2b)} = 25^{(a+14+b)}$$

   a. 22
   b. 15
   c. -22
   d. -44
   e. 14.7

13. A company has 8 applicants for a supervisor position and 7 applicants for a manager position. They need to hire 3 supervisors and 2 managers. How many combinations of individuals are possible in filling these positions if each person has an equal chance?
   a. 1176
   b. 77
   c. 40320
   d. 1100
   e. 48

14. Paul rides his scooter 25 miles in x minutes. He also rides his scooter y miles in 15 minutes at the same rate. Which of the following expressions denotes the quantity y in terms of x?
   a. $\frac{x}{375}$
   b. $\frac{x}{25}$
   c. $375x$
   d. $\frac{375}{x}$
   e. $\frac{5}{3x}$

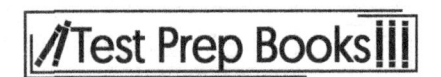

15. Student A got 85% correct on a test with 20 questions. Student B got 80% correct on a test with 25 questions. If the difference between the number of answers that Student A and Student B got correct is the same amount as the number of questions that Student C got incorrect on their test, and Student C's test had 15 questions, how many more questions did Student B answer correctly than Student C?
    a. 3 questions
    b. 8 questions
    c. 5 questions
    d. 4 questions
    e. 7 questions

16. Five of six numbers have a sum of 25. The average of all six numbers is 6. What is the sixth number?
    a. 8
    b. 12
    c. 13
    d. 10
    e. 11

17. If $x + 5 < (\sqrt{36} \times \sqrt{16}) - 3^2$, then what is the product of 3 and the greatest integer that x could be?

    a. 36
    b. 23
    c. 27
    d. 20
    e. 390

18. Simplify:

$$\frac{4a^{-1}b^3}{a^4b^{-2}} \times \frac{3a}{b}$$

   a. $12a^3b^5$
   b. $12\frac{b^4}{a^4}$
   c. $\frac{12}{a^4}$
   d. $7\frac{b^4}{a}$
   e. $4\frac{7b}{a}$

19. Mom's car drove 72 miles in 90 minutes. How fast did she drive in feet per second?
    a. 0.8 feet per second
    b. 48.9 feet per second
    c. 0.009 feet per second
    d. 70.4 feet per second
    e. 55 feet per second

20. If $n = 2^2$, and $m = n^2$, then m^n equals:
    a. 2^{12}
    b. 2^{10}
    c. 2^{18}
    d. 2^{16}
    e. 2^{20}

21. Katie ran 18 miles in 4 hours. Her rate in miles per hour is equivalent to which of the following proportions?
    a. 4 to 36
    b. 36 to 8
    c. 9 to 4
    d. 180 to 20
    e. 4 to 9

Verbal Reasoning

Reading Comprehension

Questions 1–3 are based on the following passage:

A study by the Organization for Economic Development and Cooperation of ten developing countries during the period from 1985 to 1992 found significant implementation of privatization in only three countries. The study concluded that "reductions in the central budget deficit can only be marginal" because the impact was not evaluated over several years to consider the effect of the revenues forgone from state-owned enterprises (SOEs). Several later studies measured the budgetary effects and reported significant increases in profitability and productivity as a result of privatization, but the methodological flaws related to the difficulty of isolating the performance of SOEs from other elements rendered the findings ambiguous. While the evidence on the performance of SOEs "shows that state ownership is often correlated with politicization, inefficiency, and waste of resources," the assumption that it is state ownership that creates an environment influencing the quality of performance is not proven, with the empirical research on this point having yielded conflicting results. Given the inconclusive evidence, many scholars did not concur with a World Bank statement in 1995 that SOEs "remain an important obstacle to better economic performance."

Reflecting a belief that the market is the best allocator of resources, experts have often recommended "unleashing" the private sector by removing regulations and privatizing SOEs. In 1995, to preclude hasty and simplistic privatization efforts, the World Bank recommended that SOEs be corporatized under commercial law and issued guidance on "[p]re-privatization interim measures and institutional arrangements for 'permanent SOEs.'" The bank also listed five preconditions for successful privatization: hard budget constraints; capital and labor market discipline; competition; corporate governance free of political interference; and commitment to privatization.

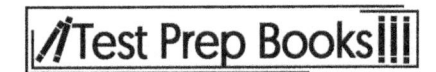

In view of the pervasive presence of SOEs in the global economy and their embodiment of political and economic considerations, SOEs are an entity to be considered and managed in the pursuit of stability.

"The State-Owned Enterprise as a Vehicle for Stability" by Neil Efird (2010), published by the Strategic Studies Institute (Department of Defense), pgs. 7–8

1. Based on the passage above, which statement can be properly inferred?
    a. State-owned enterprises always cause economic stagnation.
    b. Privatization is controversial, even among economic experts.
    c. Economic studies are always subject to intense criticism and secondhand guessing.
    d. State-owned enterprises violate commercial law.
    e. The World Bank holds the power to directly intervene in economies.

2. Which statement(s) about state-owned enterprises are true based on the passage above?
    a. The empirical research demonstrates that state-owned enterprises are efficient and productive.
    b. Developing countries have little influence on the World Bank's policies.
    c. Privatization enjoys widespread popular support wherever it is implemented.
    d. State-owned enterprises do not have sizable effects on the global economy.
    e. For privatization to be successful, politics should not intrude in the governance of corporations.

3. Which statement most accurately identifies the author's ultimate conclusion?
    a. The market is the best allocator of resources, so private enterprises will always outperform state-owned enterprises.
    b. The World Bank holds considerable expertise in matters related to state-owned enterprises and privatization.
    c. State-owned enterprises should be managed in a way that promotes economic stability, which might require a measured approach to privatization.
    d. Studies conducted with a flawed methodology should not be the basis for economic decisions.
    e. State-owned enterprises should be privatized under commercial law as long as the government adheres to the five preconditions for privatization.

Questions 4 and 5 are based on the following passage:

Despite spending far more on health care than any other nation, the United States ranks near the bottom on key health indicators. This paradox has been attributed to underinvestment in addressing social and behavioral determinants of health. A recent Institute of Medicine (IOM) report linked the shorter overall life expectancy in the United States to problems that are either caused by behavioral risks (e.g., injuries and homicides, adolescent pregnancy and sexually transmitted infections (STIs), HIV/AIDS, drug-related deaths, lung diseases, obesity, and diabetes) or affected by social conditions (e.g., birth outcomes, heart disease, and disability).

While spending more than other countries per capita on healthcare services, the United States spends less on average than do other nations on social services impacting social and behavioral determinants of health. Bradley, et al., found that Organization for Economic Co-operation and Development (OECD) nations with a higher ratio of spending on social services relative to healthcare services have better health and longer life expectancies than do those like the United States that have a lower ratio.

Practice Test #2

The Clinical & Translational Science Awards (CTSAs) established by the National Institutes of Health (NIH) have helped initiate interdisciplinary programs in more than sixty institutions that aim to advance the translation of research findings from "bench" to "bedside" to "community." Social and behavioral issues are inherent aspects of the translation of findings at the bench into better care and better health. Insofar as Clinical and Translational Science Institutes (CTSIs) will be evaluated for renewal—not only on the basis of their bench science discoveries, but also by their ability to move these discoveries into practice and improve individual and population health—the CTSIs should be motivated to include social and behavioral scientists in their work.

Population Health: Behavioral and Social Science Insights, Robert M. Kaplan et al. (2015), published by the Agency for Healthcare Research and Quality (National Institutes of Health), "Determinants of Health and Longevity" by Nancy E. Adler and Aric A. Prather, excerpted from pages 411 and 417

4. Which statement describes how the United States differs in its approach to health care compared with other nations?
    a. On average, the United States spends more on social services impacting social and behavioral determinants of health than other nations.
    b. Compared with other nations, the United States has a higher ratio of spending on social services relative to healthcare services.
    c. Compared with other nations, the United States spends more per capita on healthcare services despite producing worse health outcomes.
    d. Compared with other nations, the United States has a lower life expectancy due to its lack of spending on healthcare services.
    e. Unlike other nations, the United States doesn't fund interdisciplinary programs that include behavioral and social science.

5. Which statement(s) most accurately identifies the author's main thesis?
    a. Despite outspending other countries on health care, the United States performs poorly on key health indicators.
    b. The National Institutes of Health created the Clinical and Translational Science Awards to develop interdisciplinary programs in more than sixty institutions.
    c. Social and behavioral factors are an underappreciated aspect of health, and if they are better understood and properly addressed, health outcomes will improve.
    d. The United States has the shortest overall life expectancy in the world due to unaddressed behavioral risks and deteriorating social conditions.
    e. Life expectancy is the most important healthcare indicator because it encapsulates every other relevant factor.

Questions 6–9 are based on the following passage:

Leonardo da Vinci was a revolutionary artist whose contributions indelibly changed how artists viewed the connection between science, philosophy, and art. His works went beyond the traditional painting techniques through the inclusion of anatomy and geometry. He became a major contributor to the Italian Renaissance, and his work established him as one of the greatest polymaths in history.

Da Vinci was deeply interested in human anatomy, and this can be seen in his art. His study of the human body went so far as dissecting cadavers in order to better understand the inner workings of the body. He wanted to understand the structure of muscles and tendons and to understand how things moved within the body. This led to incredibly accurate figure drawings that had never been seen before. His art conveyed the fluidity that the human form is capable of as well as the expressive nature of movement.

Da Vinci's skills of observation and replication were showcased not only through his depiction of human anatomy, but also in his art's perspective, light, and form. His composition was unlike anything that the art world had seen before. He brought a degree of realism to his art that very accurately replicated the natural world. This laid the foundation for more modern techniques that artists have continued to use for centuries.

One unique technique that da Vinci employed is known as *sfumato*. This is a method of blending colors and tones with soft transitions. The key to this technique involved a keen eye for the play between light and shadow as well as subtlety in depicting these transitions without using harsh lines. *Sfumato* comes from the Italian word for smoke, *fumo*. The word encapsulates the hazy, soft quality of the technique, which lends paintings an atmospheric quality that creates depth and mood. It was considered to be a groundbreaking innovation for Renaissance artists. The technique can most famously be seen in da Vinci's *Mona Lisa* painting.

6. Why does the passage most likely mention da Vinci's practice of dissecting cadavers?
    a. To explain the way that da Vinci's methods differed from his peers and explain why he was more successful because of it
    b. To highlight da Vinci's interest in the morbidity of human death
    c. To emphasize da Vinci's dedication to understanding the human body as a foundation for his art
    d. To provide historical context for the complexity of medical research during the Renaissance period

7. According to the passage, which of the following statements about *sfumato* is true?
    a. It was a groundbreaking method that added depth and mood to art.
    b. It was unpopular with Renaissance period artists due to how difficult it was to execute.
    c. It works best in geometric artwork that requires contrast and precision.
    d. It was too soft of a method for the Renaissance artists who preferred to create dramatic art.

8. Which of the following examples most closely aligns with da Vinci's method of combining art and science?
    a. A video game artist who generates generic virtual environments before adding their own detailed assets
    b. An agriculturalist who studies which varieties of insects are killing the most crops before choosing which pesticide to use
    c. A botanist who studies leaf vein patterns and takes samples to use for reference when they later illustrate them for educational textbooks
    d. An architect who aims to revive traditional styles that have been forgone in favor of modern techniques

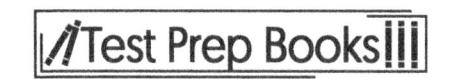

9. Which of the following best describes the function of the second paragraph?
   a. To explain da Vinci's philosophy on the importance of art imitating life as closely as possible
   b. To introduce the topic of da Vinci's contributions to geometry and how it changed abstract art forever
   c. To shift the discussion from da Vinci's artistic accomplishments to his scientific success
   d. To provide insight into how da Vinci's anatomical studies informed his realistic portrayal of the human form

Questions 10–13 are based on the following passage:

Exoplanets are planets that orbit stars outside of our solar system. The first exoplanet was confirmed in 1992, and thousands have been identified since. Exoplanets are particularly interesting as they have sparked conversations as to the possibility of life on other planets.

Exoplanets vary greatly in their composition and characteristics. Some are gaseous bodies similar to Jupiter while others are larger versions of Earth. Exoplanets' distance from their stars can vary greatly, and that distance affects the temperature and habitability of the exoplanet. Scientists work hard to determine which exoplanets orbit in the habitable zone, which allows for liquid water to exist. The presence of liquid water is a key sign that the exoplanet may be able to support life.

Astronomers can detect exoplanets through the use of the transit method, which was first successful in 1999. The transit method employs telescopes to monitor stars for dips in brightness, which are usually caused by a planet passing in front of the star. Additionally, scientists search for biosignatures, which are chemical signs of life such as the presence of oxygen or methane.

Studying exoplanets requires the use of advanced technology. The Keplar Space Telescope, the James Webb Space Telescope, and NASA's TESS (Transiting Exoplanet Survey Satellite) Space Telescope have all enabled scientists to detect thousands of exoplanets that were previously undiscovered. One can only imagine the discoveries mankind will continue to make as technology continues to advance.

10. Based on the passage, which of the following exoplanets would be the most interesting to scientists?
    a. A rocky planet that is extremely close to the star it orbits
    b. A planet orbiting near its star and containing bodies of water
    c. A gaseous planet composed of methane and no oxygen
    d. A planet that has no atmosphere and is orbiting at a great distance from its star

11. Which of the following is an inference that can be made about the transit method?
    a. It is an outdated method of looking for exoplanets and needs to be retired.
    b. It would not be an effective method in an area without stars.
    c. It is less reliable than searching for biosignatures to detect exoplanets.
    d. It is the only possible method for finding exoplanets.

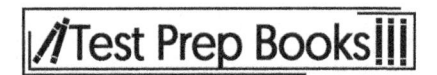

12. What is most likely to be the reason the passage mentions the Kepler Space Telescope, James Webb Space Telescope, and NASA's TESS Space Telescope?
    a. To argue that the current technology is not performing adequately to discover exoplanets
    b. To compare the accomplishments of the various telescopes
    c. To emphasize the need for advanced technology when discovering exoplanets
    d. To suggest that telescopes are not an effective way to identify exoplanets

13. Which word best describes the author's attitude toward the future technological advancements for space exploration?
    a. Distrustful
    b. Neutral
    c. Skeptical
    d. Hopeful

Critical Reasoning

14. Teacher: Students don't need parental involvement to succeed. In my class of twenty kids, the two highest achieving students come from foster homes. There are too many children in the foster homes for their parents to monitor homework and enforce study habits. It's always the case that students can overcome their parents' indifference.
What mistake does the teacher commit in his reasoning?
    a. The teacher incorrectly applies a common rule.
    b. The teacher's conclusion is totally unjustified.
    c. The teacher relies on an unreasonably small sample size in drawing his conclusion.
    d. The teacher fails to consider competing theories.
    e. The teacher is biased.

15. Trent is a member of the SWAT Team, the most elite tactical unit at the city's police department. SWAT apprehends more suspected criminals than all other police units combined. Taken as a whole, the police department solves a higher percentage of crime than ever before in its history. Within the SWAT team, Trent's four-man unit is the most successful. However, the number of unsolved crime increases every year.
Which of the following statements, if true, most logically resolves the apparent paradox?
    a. Trent's SWAT team is the city's best police unit.
    b. Violent crime has decreased dramatically, while petty drug offenses have increased substantially.
    c. The total number of crimes increases every year.
    d. Aside from the SWAT units, the police department is largely incompetent.
    e. The police department focuses more on crimes involving serious injury or significant property damage.

16. West Korea's economy is experiencing high rates of growth for the sixth consecutive quarter. An autocratic despot dominates all aspects of West Korean society, and as a result, West Koreans enjoy less civil liberties and freedom than neighboring countries. Clearly, civil liberties do not impact economic gains.

The following, if true, strengthens the argument, EXCEPT:
   a. Neighboring countries' democratic processes are often deadlocked and unable to respond to immediate economic problems.
   b. The autocratic despot started governing the country six quarters ago.
   c. West Korea found a massive oil reserve under the country shortly before the autocratic despot seized power.
   d. Political protests in neighboring countries often shorten workdays and limit productivity.
   e. The West Korean autocratic despot devotes all of his time to solving economic problems.

17. Sociologist: Marriage is one of the most important societal institutions. The marital relationship provides numerous structural benefits for married couples and their offspring. Studies consistently show that children born out of wedlock are less likely to attend college and more likely to work low-paying jobs. Additionally, married people are more likely to be homeowners and save for retirement. Therefore, if marriage rates decline, _____.

Which one of the following is most logically the sociologist's assumption?
   a. society will collapse.
   b. everyone would have less money.
   c. nobody would own homes.
   d. people would be happier.
   e. college attendance would probably decline.

18. Economist: Countries with lower tax rates tend to have stronger economies. Although higher taxes raise more revenue, highly taxed consumers have less disposable income. An economy can never grow if consumers aren't able to purchase goods and services. Therefore, the government should lower tax rates across the board.

The economist's argument depends on assuming that:
   a. The top five world economies have the lowest tax rates in the world.
   b. Consumers' disposable income is directly related to their ability to purchase goods and services.
   c. Lower tax rates will be much more popular with consumers.
   d. Increasing disposable income is the only way to ensure economic growth.
   e. Economic growth is more important than supporting social welfare programs.

19. Zookeeper: Big cats are undoubtedly among the smartest land mammals. Lions, tigers, and jaguars immediately adjust to their new surroundings. Other animals refuse to eat or drink in captivity, but the big cats relish their timely prepared meals. Big cats never attempt to escape their enclosures.

Which one of the following, if true, most weakens the zookeeper's argument?
   a. Big cats don't attempt to escape because they can't figure out their enclosures' weak spots.
   b. No qualified expert believes that adjusting to captivity is a measure of intelligence.
   c. Bears also do not have any trouble adjusting to captivity.
   d. A recent study comparing the brain scans of large mammals revealed that big cats exhibit the most brain activity when stimulated.
   e. Zoos devote exponentially more resources to big cats relative to other animals.

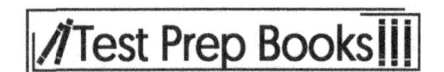

20. A town council argues that the implementation of a new campaign to increase the use of the recycling program in the last quarter of the year is the sole reason for the 25 percent reduction in yearly landfill waste. They point to the weekly pickup of recycling bins and the educational flyers on reducing, reusing, and recycling as key initiatives in this campaign. The council believes that these initiatives will lead to long-term waste reduction.

Which of the following would weaken the town council's argument?
   a. A survey showed that many residents are not yet aware of the program's existence.
   b. Local environmental groups have released studies showing that similar recycling campaigns alone reduced landfill waste by at least 25 percent.
   c. Many households have reported that they feel more inclined to recycle now that they have dedicated bins.
   d. Many residents reported that they had already begun recycling earlier in the year, before the new campaign was implemented.
   e. The town's population significantly increased prior to the implementation of the recycling campaign.

21. Maria runs a small coffee shop. Her investors have recently informed her that the sales revenue for the shop has declined over the past few months. They are pressuring Maria to determine the potential cause for the decline so that it can be properly addressed. Maria argues that the decline is due to factors such as poor location and a lack of advertising rather than to low customer satisfaction.

Which of the following would strengthen Maria's argument?
   a. Online reviews for Maria's coffee shop over the last few months have been mixed with about half being negative and half being positive.
   b. A local report stated that many small businesses in the area are being forced to reduce their advertising budgets due to rising rent costs.
   c. A survey of nearby neighborhoods revealed that 60 percent of residents were unaware of the coffee shop's existence.
   d. Sales at competing coffee shops in the area have remained steady despite similar product offerings and prices.
   e. The coffee shop recently needed extensive repairs to its roof totaling $10,000, which has cut into profits.

Practice Test #2

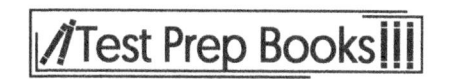

22. Janet is a school counselor, and she believes that the rise in mental health issues among teenagers is primarily due to social media use rather than academic pressure. She points to studies linking excessive screen time to heightened anxiety and depression rates. Janet argues that if schools implement programs to educate students about healthy social media habits, they can mitigate these negative effects and improve overall mental well-being, thus leading to better school performance regardless of academic stressors.

Which of the following would strengthen Janet's argument?
   a. Teens report that having less intensive homework every night leads to lowered stress levels.
   b. A survey of school employees showed that students who stay off of their phone during class perform better on exams.
   c. A recent study shows that teens who reduce their time on social media have an easier time sleeping and focusing on schoolwork.
   d. Social media that is used for educational purposes can help to engage students more than traditional teaching methods.
   e. Students who feel stressed due to academic pressure are more likely to share their struggles online than with a school counselor.

23. Joana heard that drinking a cup of green tea every day greatly improves health due to green tea's high antioxidant content. She has been drinking a cup of green tea every day for 6 months and has not been sick once during this time. Joana concludes that the theory about green tea is accurate and that everyone should drink green tea daily to maintain good health.

Which of the following best weakens Joana's argument?
   a. Joana substituted green tea with white tea for 5 days during the 6 month period.
   b. Joana's friends drink green tea but occasionally fall ill.
   c. Joana has always had a strong immune system and has only fallen ill a few times in her life.
   d. There are many varieties of tea that contain antioxidants, not just green tea.
   e. Joana has been spending more time outdoors to improve her mental well-being.

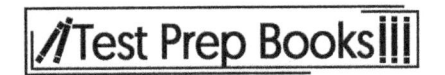

Data Insights

Multi-Source Reasoning

Set 1
Tab 1

The city of Austin, TX, has seen a steady increase in population over the course of the last decade. From 2014 to 2024, the population increased from 500,000 to 650,000.

Year	Population
2014	500,000
2015	524,352
2016	536,275
2017	548,225
2018	557,369
2019	571,424
2020	588,261
2021	593,975
2022	617,286
2023	639,212
2024	650,000

Tab 2

For 2024, the national employment rate was 90%, and the local employment rate in Austin, TX, was 95%. The following chart shows the percentage of the employed population that work in service, manufacturing, and other industries.

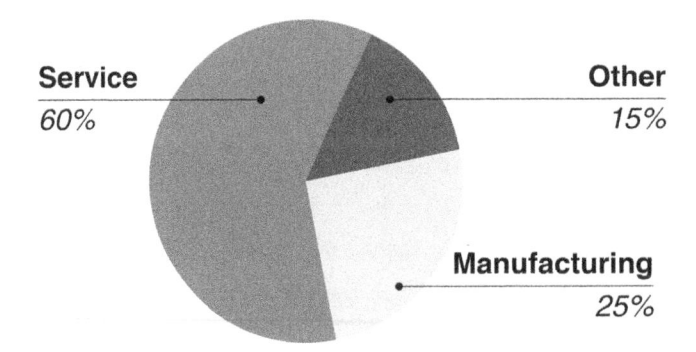

Service 60%
Other 15%
Manufacturing 25%

Practice Test #2

Tab 3

The mean income for citizens in Austin, TX, in 2024 was $45,000, with 30% of citizens earning less than $30,000, 50% earning between $30,000 and $70,000, and 20% earning more than $70,000 per year.

1. Between 2014 and 2024, what was the compound annual growth rate (CAGR) for Austin, TX?
    a. 2.4%
    b. 2.9%
    c. 2.7%
    d. 3.6%
    e. 3.9%

2. Check either Yes or No for each of the following statements:

Yes	No	
○	○	The mean annual population increase between 2017 and 2023 was 15,164.5.
○	○	162,500 people were employed in the manufacturing industry in Austin in 2024.
○	○	If the population in 2025 is expected to be 2.5% higher than it was in 2024, but the statistics for income remain the same, the number of people making less than $30,000 will be greater than 200,000.

3. Based on of the provided information, which of the following statements would be considered accurate?

   I. Most employed citizens in Austin, TX, work in the service industry.

   II. Most citizens in Austin, TX, earn more than $70,000 annually.

   III. The number of unemployed people in 2024 was more than triple the amount by which the population increased from 2023 to 2024.

   IV. Between 2018 and 2021, the mean population of Austin was 589,502.

   V. At least half of the citizens in Austin, TX, earn between $30,000 and $70,000 annually.

   a. I, II, III
   b. I, III, IV
   c. I, II, V
   d. I, III, V
   e. All of the above

Set 2

Tab 1

A clothing company sells pants, shirts, skirts, dresses, and shorts. The sales numbers for each product have risen by 2.5% each year. Based on its sales predictions, the company has produced 0.5% more of each garment than it has sold each year, and the leftover garments get donated to the company's charity organization to give clothing to people in need. Additionally, the company donates 1.5% of the cost of each garment to an outside charity that works to give meals to the homeless. The number sold of each of these articles of clothing in 2024 is represented by the following graph:

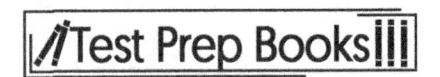

	Pants	Shirts	Skirts	Dresses	Shorts
Number sold	9,342	10,211	4,129	3,240	7,857

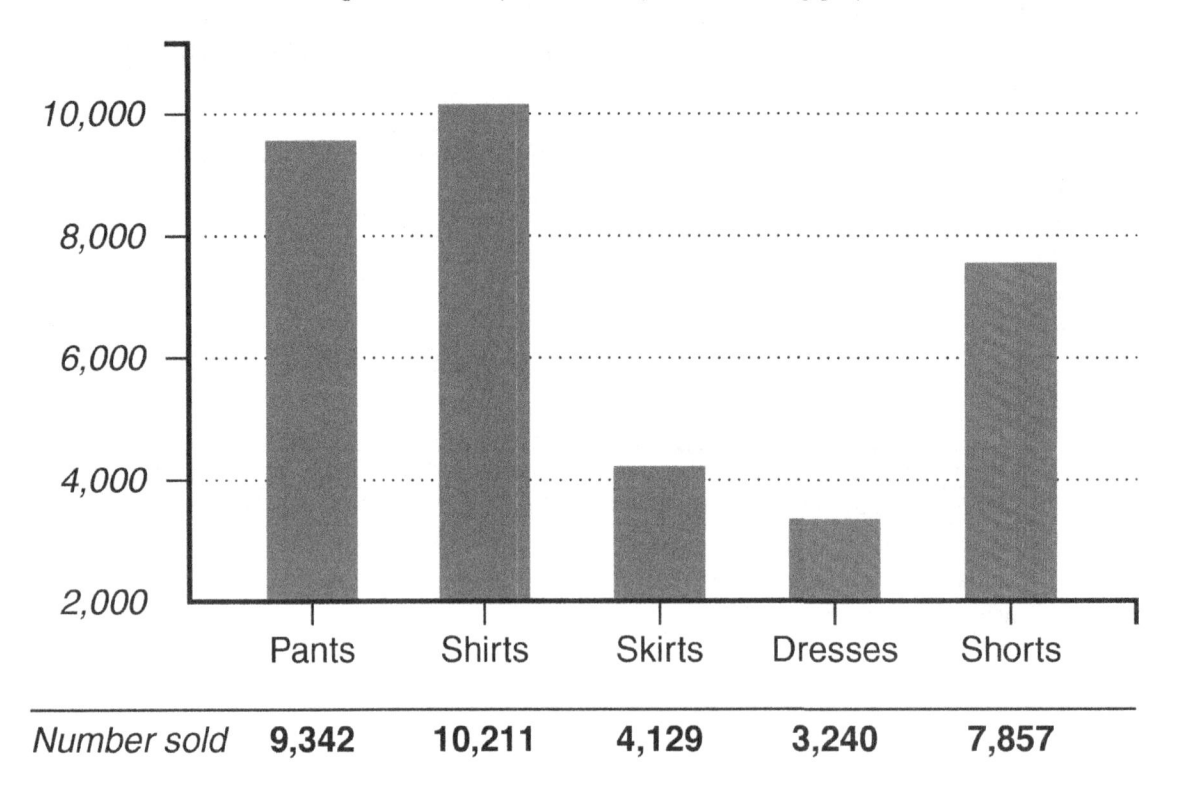

Tab 2

The prices for each type of garment in 2024 are represented by the following table. Additionally, the production cost of each item in 2024 accounts for 17.4% of the price of each item.

Product	Price
Pants	$59.99
Shirts	$35.50
Skirts	$40.25
Dresses	$72.75
Shorts	$25.99

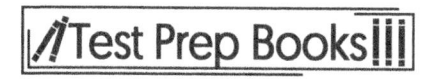

Tab 3

The company has raised the prices of products over the years. In addition to this, the cost of producing each item has gone up by 1.7% each year for the past 5 years. The following table shows the percent increase in price for all products sold each year for the past 5 years:

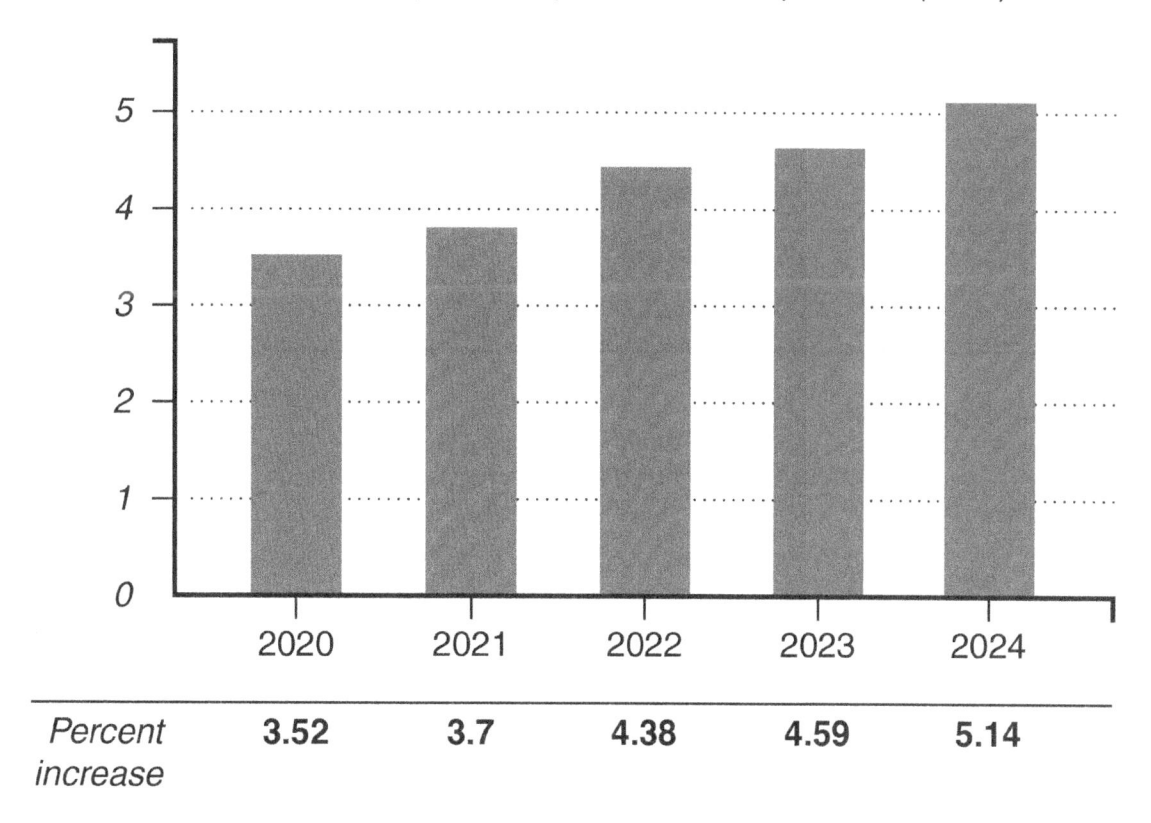

	2020	2021	2022	2023	2024
Percent increase	3.52	3.7	4.38	4.59	5.14

4. How much money did the clothing company make from selling pants in 2023?
   a. $575,945.50
   b. $478,239.25
   c. $386,465.33
   d. $487,935.24
   e. $520,044.84

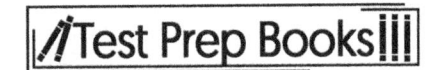

5. Check either Yes or No for each of the following statements:

Yes	No	
○	○	The garment associated with the median cost of the types of clothes from this company in 2024 is a skirt.
○	○	The company made less than $275,000 from selling shirts in 2021.
○	○	If prices go up by 6.5% by 2025, the cost of dresses will be more than $75.50 per dress.

6. Check either Yes or No for each of the following statements:

Yes	No	
○	○	The combined cost per item to produce shorts and skirts in 2024 was less than the cost to produce dresses per item.
○	○	The mean price increase from 2020 to 2023 was 4.05%.
○	○	The amount of money that went to charity organizations from pants sales in 2024 was $8,125.50.

Graphics Interpretation

7. The following graph represents the salary distribution across different departments within a national paper distributor:

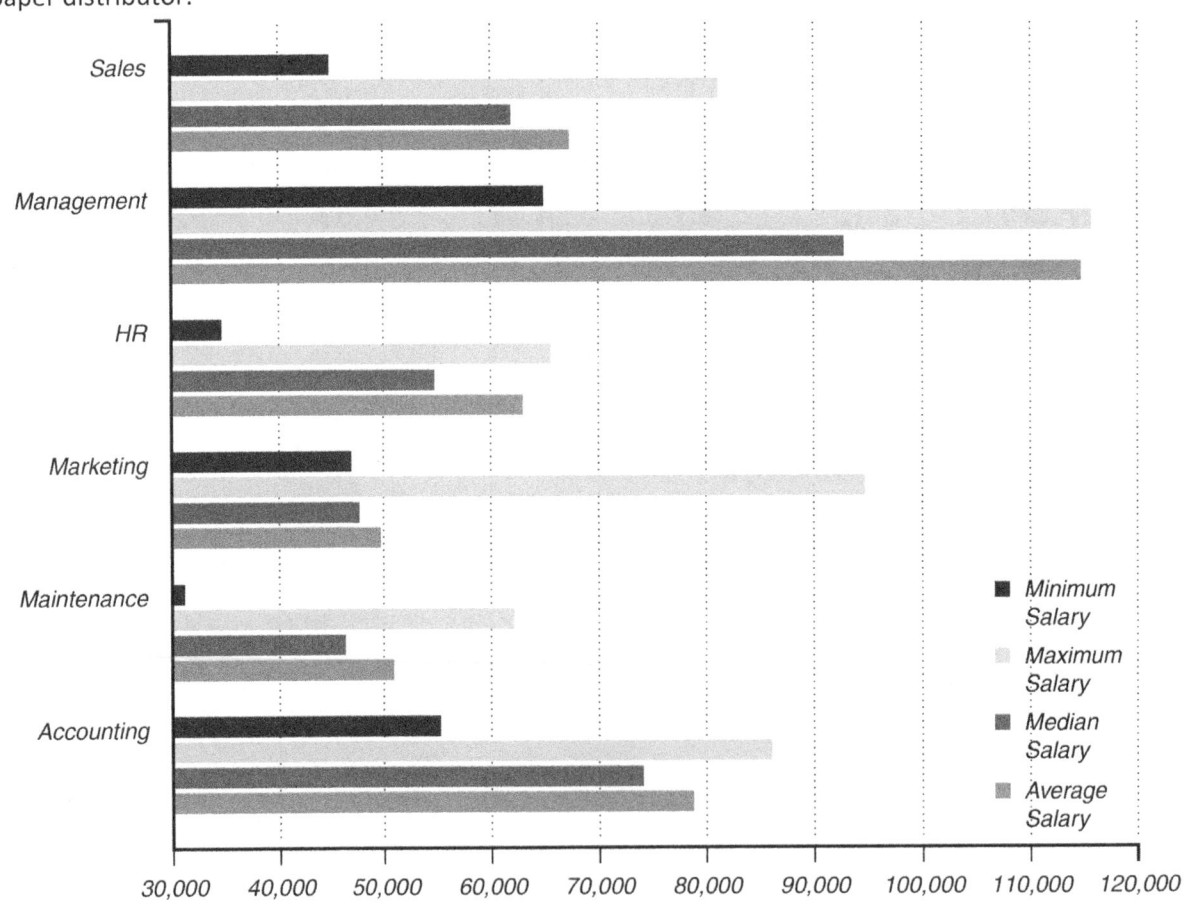

Based on the information in the graph, fill in the blanks:
The approximate value of the range for salaries in the HR department is _____.
   a. $31,000
   b. $39,000
   c. $45,000
   d. $53,000

The difference between the maximum salary in Sales and the minimum salary in the Maintenance department is _____.
   a. $12,000
   b. $26,000
   c. $31,000
   d. $50,000

8. A survey was conducted to see how often moms and dads choose to feed their babies a certain brand of mashed peas. The answer choices were never, <10 times per month, 10–20 times per month, and >20 times per month. A total of 500 survey participants were divided equally into 2 categories, moms and dads.

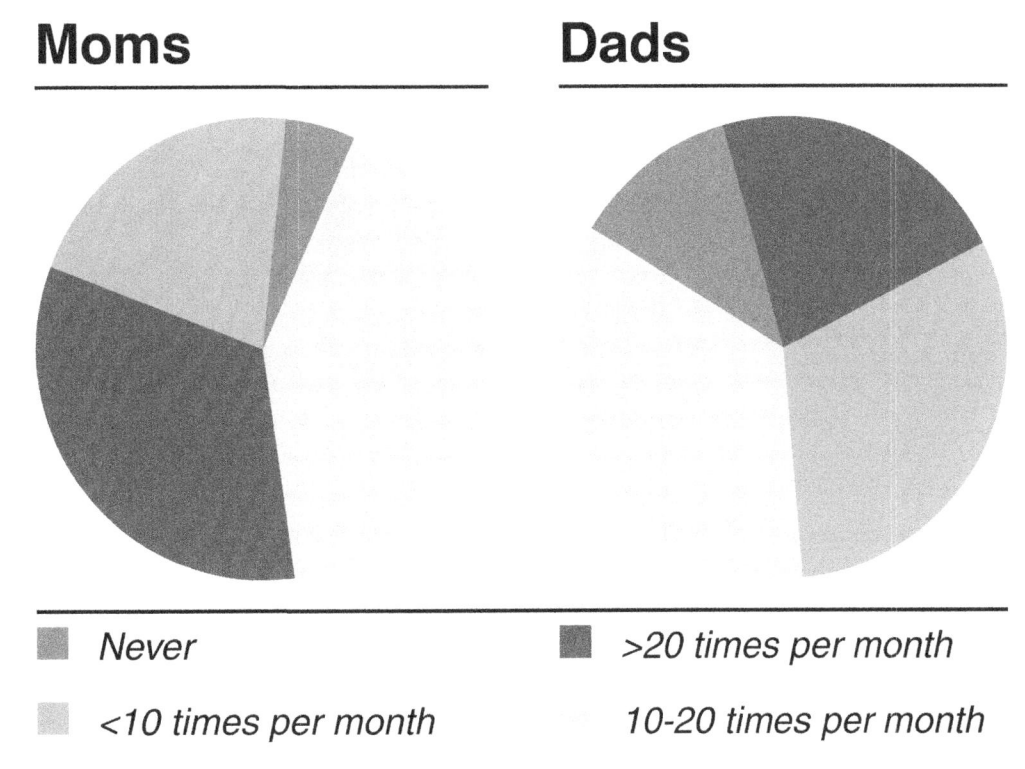

Moms | **Dads**

- Never
- <10 times per month
- >20 times per month
- 10-20 times per month

Based on the information in the graphs, fill in the blanks:
The percentage of dads who feed their babies the mashed peas less than 10 times per month is _____ than the percentage of moms who never feed their babies the peas.
   a. 5% more
   b. 25% more
   c. 5% less
   d. 15% less

123

The total percentage of moms who feed their babies the peas at least 10 times per month is _____ than the percentage of dads who feed their babies the peas zero to less than 10 times per month.

a. 10% less
b. 50% less
c. 30% more
d. 75% more

9. A school recorded the average grades of 10 students, each represented by the numbers 1–10, over the course of 2 semesters last year. Additionally, the average number of hours spent studying each week per student was reported.

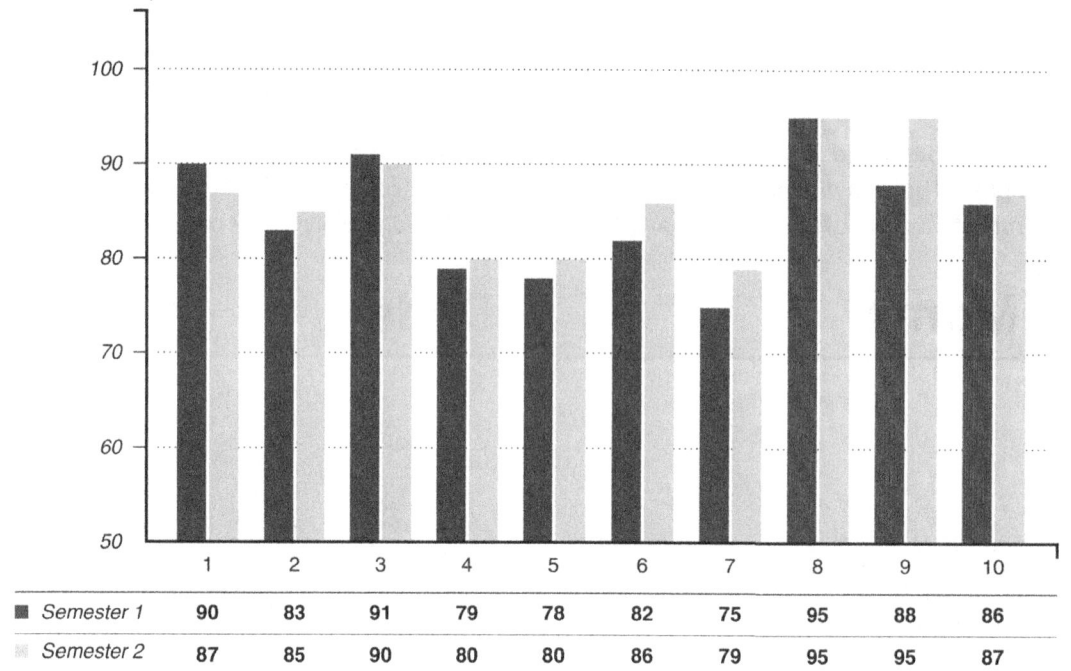

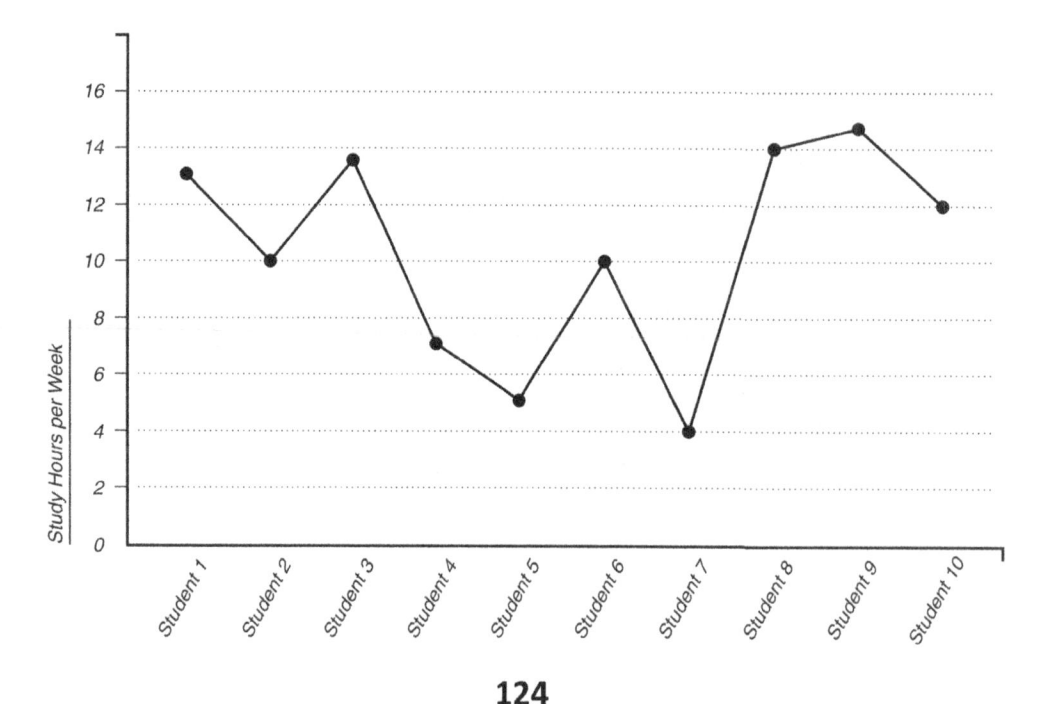

	1	2	3	4	5	6	7	8	9	10
Semester 1	90	83	91	79	78	82	75	95	88	86
Semester 2	87	85	90	80	80	86	79	95	95	87

Practice Test #2

Based on the information provided in the graphs, fill in the blanks:
The correlation between hours spent studying and academic performance is a _____.
   a. Strong positive
   b. Weak positive
   c. Weak negative
   d. Strong negative

Of all the students, _____ showed the largest range in grade performance between the first and second semesters.
   a. Student 3
   b. Student 7
   c. Student 9
   d. Student 10

10. An advertising company has kept a record of the website traffic for 5 clients over the course of 2023. The traffic for all sites is up 5.7% from 2022, and projections indicate that traffic will have risen on each site by 6.2% by the time data is in for 2024. The following graph shows the monthly site traffic for each client over the course of 2023:

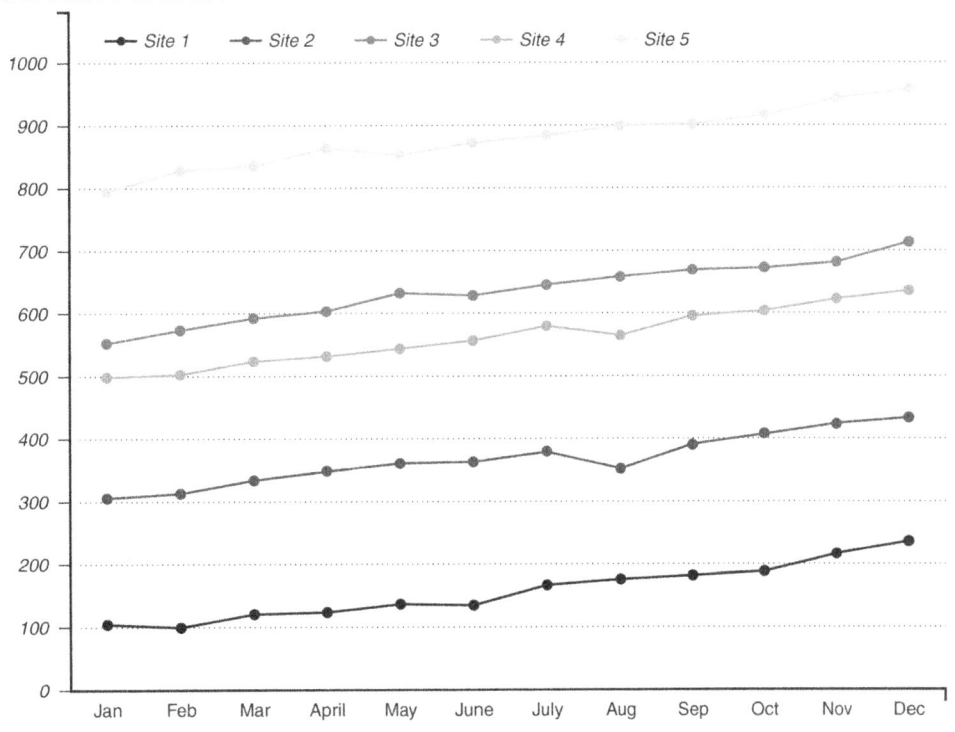

Based on the information in the graph, fill in the blanks:
The percentage increase of Site 2 between July and October was _____ than the percentage increase of Site 3 from January through April.
   a. 2.42% less
   b. 5.97% less
   c. 2.48% more
   d. 5.76% more

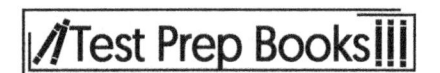

The difference between the highest and lowest values in the range for site traffic between February and June is _____.

a. 570
b. 625
c. 650
d. 770

Two-Part Analysis

Read each passage and answer the question at the end of each passage by marking the appropriate answers for each column:

11. At the state university, there are 1,350 business majors. There are 3 times as many marketing majors as accounting majors, and there are 50 students who are double majors in both accounting and marketing. The state university offers no other business degrees. Which number of accounting majors and which number of marketing majors are consistent with this information?

Make one selection for each column:

Accounting	Marketing	
○	○	a. 350
○	○	b. 250
○	○	c. 1,050
○	○	d. 1,150

12. There is a small village in the countryside that is home to a farmer named Drew. In Drew's fields, there are five types of plants that each need to be tended to in their own specific manner. These plants are basil, carrots, cucumbers, lettuce, and tomatoes. Each day, Drew follows a specific schedule to tend to all of his different plants. The tomato must always be watered first, the cucumber is never tended immediately after the lettuce, the basil is only ever watered right before the carrots, and the lettuce is never tended after the basil. Finally, the carrots are always tended to last. Drew always sticks to his schedule, and he is determined to keep it the same each day to get to each plant in its proper order. Which plant is tended to third, and which is tended to fourth?

Make one selection for each column:

Tended 3rd	Tended 4th	
○	○	a. Basil
○	○	b. Carrots
○	○	c. Cucumbers
○	○	d. Lettuce
○	○	e. Tomatoes

Practice Test #2

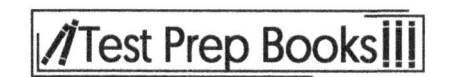

Table Analysis

13. A multinational computer software company operates on 4 continents. The following table displays its quarterly sales (in millions) for the years of 2021 through the first quarter of 2024 in all 4 regions.

Year	Quarter	North America	South America	Asia	Europe
2021	Q1	$122.24	$82.24	$112.41	$94.33
2021	Q2	$120.39	$80.97	$110.82	$100.86
2021	Q3	$111.41	$84.23	$125.44	$98.67
2021	Q4	$130.49	$92.96	$120.72	$106.43
2022	Q1	$129.54	$89.19	$131.33	$104.21
2022	Q2	$134.55	$91.22	$133.94	$124.99
2022	Q3	$135.97	$99.61	$125.82	$114.65
2022	Q4	$132.11	$100.88	$138.24	$131.83
2023	Q1	$147.69	$104.62	$144.77	$135.29
2023	Q2	$144.32	$110.93	$140.13	$139.20
2023	Q3	$175.93	$121.95	$156.21	$144.97
2023	Q4	$161.24	$118.86	$170.74	$143.92
2024	Q1	$160.36	$117.28	$165.27	$150.21

Choose either Yes or No for each of the following statements:

Yes	No	
○	○	The average growth rate per quarter in North America was greater than 2.5% between Q4 2021 and Q2 2022.
○	○	The median amount for quarterly sales in Asia between Q1 2021 and Q1 2024 was $133.94.
○	○	The average sales in Europe between Q4 2022 and Q3 2023 were less than the average sales in South America between Q4 2022 and Q3 2023.

14. A farm has kept track of its production (in tons) of okra, corn, soybeans, rice, wheat, and tobacco over the course of the past year. Production rates have grown 1.25% each year for the past 5 years. The following table represents the farm's monthly production of each crop for 2023.

Month	Okra	Corn	Soybeans	Rice	Tobacco
January	1.2	7.3	12.2	8.4	6.1
February	1.4	8.7	8.1	6.2	4.5
March	1.7	9.5	7.9	7.9	3.2
April	1.8	10.4	8.4	8.7	4.7
May	2.1	16.9	9.1	9.5	5.4
June	3.4	17.3	10.6	12.2	8.1
July	5.2	20.2	12.3	13.1	9.8
August	6.4	21.4	14.8	14.7	11.4
September	4.2	25.7	20.1	13.9	13.1
October	3.1	24.3	22.5	12.6	12.6
November	1.8	19.2	21.7	10.7	10.2
December	1.1	18.4	17.9	9.1	8.6

Choose either Yes or No for each of the following statements:

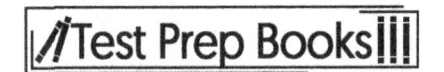

Yes	No	
○	○	The total production of corn for the year in 2023 was more than the total production of soybeans in 2021.
○	○	The amount of corn produced in October was less than double the median for soybeans for the year.
○	○	The average amount of tobacco grown between June and December of 2023 was 55.46 tons more than the amount of rice grown between January and July.

15. The following table represents the rainfall (in inches) in 2023 for various cities around the world, as well as their number of rainy days, driest months, and wettest months. Rainfall has increased for all of these cities by 0.05 inches each year for the past 50 years.

City	Rainfall (inches)	# of Rainy Days	Wettest Month	Driest Month
New York	51.6	124	April	February
London	64.4	145	October	February
Tokyo	24.3	110	June	December
Sydney	41.2	128	March	September
Mumbai	94.1	76	July	January
Cairo	2.8	6	January	June
Paris	27.5	97	December	March
Beijing	32.9	82	July	January
São Paulo	57.7	104	January	August
Cape Town	19.2	58	June	February

Choose either Yes or No for each of the following statements:

Yes	No	
○	○	The amount of rainfall in Mumbai in 2023 was more than 30% of the total rainfall for all of these cities in 2023.
○	○	The ratio of rainfall to the number of rainy days for the year in London in 2023 was at least 65% more than the ratio of rainfall to rainy days in Paris.
○	○	The city with the third highest number of rainy days also has the third highest amount of rainfall per year.

Practice Test #2

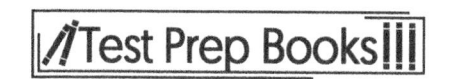

Data Sufficiency

Decide whether the data given in the statements are sufficient to answer the question.

16. A financial advisor is performing an analysis of two investment portfolios, Portfolio A and Portfolio B, to determine which is the better option to recommend to one of their top clients. Does Portfolio A show a greater annual return than Portfolio B?

   Statement 1: The financial advisor found that the annual return on Portfolio A was 5.7%.

   Statement 2: They also found that the annual return on Portfolio B was 2.3% more than twice the annual return on Portfolio A.

   a. Statement (1) ALONE is sufficient, but Statement (2) ALONE is not sufficient.
   b. Statement (2) ALONE is sufficient, but Statement (1) ALONE is not sufficient.
   c. BOTH statements TOGETHER are sufficient, but NEITHER statement ALONE is sufficient.
   d. EACH statement ALONE is sufficient.
   e. Statements (1) and (2) TOGETHER are not sufficient.

17. The plant manager at a local textile plant wants to compare the efficiency of two pieces of equipment. Is Machine A more efficient than Machine B?

   Statement 1: The manager found that, every hour, Machine A consumes 46.2 kWh of energy and produces 84 units.

   Statement 2: They also found that Machine B consumes 54.7 kWh of energy per hour.

   a. Statement (1) ALONE is sufficient, but Statement (2) ALONE is not sufficient.
   b. Statement (2) ALONE is sufficient, but Statement (1) ALONE is not sufficient.
   c. BOTH statements TOGETHER are sufficient, but NEITHER statement ALONE is sufficient.
   d. EACH statement ALONE is sufficient.
   e. Statements (1) and (2) TOGETHER are not sufficient.

18. Katie and Serena are writing a story for a newspaper. Katie can write at a speed 2 times faster than Serena can. How long will it take them to finish the story while working together?

   1) Working individually, Katie could finish the story in 4 hours.

   2) Serena can write 1,500 words per hour.

   a. Statement (1) ALONE is sufficient, but statement (2) ALONE is NOT sufficient.
   b. Statement (2) ALONE is sufficient, but statement (1) ALONE is NOT sufficient.
   c. BOTH statements TOGETHER are sufficient, but NEITHER statement ALONE is sufficient.
   d. EACH statement ALONE is sufficient.
   e. Statements (1) and (2) TOGETHER are NOT sufficient.

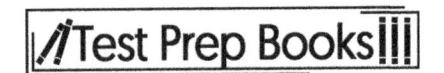

19. To stock your grocery store, you purchase boxes of oatmeal from your supplier for $2 each and sell them to customers. How much do you individually sell them for?

   1) Your profit from each sale is 25%.

   2) The amount that you pay for the oatmeal is 80% of what you sell it for.

   a. Statement (1) ALONE is sufficient, but statement (2) ALONE is NOT sufficient.
   b. Statement (2) ALONE is sufficient, but statement (1) ALONE is NOT sufficient.
   c. BOTH statements TOGETHER are sufficient, but NEITHER statement ALONE is sufficient.
   d. EACH statement ALONE is sufficient.
   e. Statements (1) and (2) TOGETHER are NOT sufficient.

20. A set consists of the total snowfall for 7 days. Is the median of the set less than the mode?

   1) The mean and median of the set are equal to 3.

   2) The mode appears twice in the set.

   a. Statement (1) ALONE is sufficient, but statement (2) ALONE is NOT sufficient.
   b. Statement (2) ALONE is sufficient, but statement (1) ALONE is NOT sufficient.
   c. BOTH statements TOGETHER are sufficient, but NEITHER statement ALONE is sufficient.
   d. EACH statement ALONE is sufficient.
   e. Statements (1) and (2) TOGETHER are NOT sufficient.

Answer Explanations #2

Quantitative Reasoning

1. C: First, there are 5 different types of fruit baskets sold that contain only one type of fruit. Each basket can have either a ribbon or a balloon, so there are actually $2 \times 5 = 10$ types. For the second type of basket, there are 4 out of the 5 possible types of fruit in each basket. Order does not matter, so this is a combination:

$$C_4^5 = \frac{5 \times 4 \times 3 \times 2}{4 \times 3 \times 2 \times 1} = 5.$$

To account for the option of either a ribbon or a balloon, multiply this amount by 2 to obtain 10. Therefore, there are 20 different types of fruit baskets.

2. A: In order to determine the correct choice, we can select values for the integers, plug them into each expression, and compare. Let $c = 3, b = 4$, and $a = 5$. Therefore,

$$a(b + c) = 5(4 + 3) = 35, b(a + c) = 4(5 + 3) = 32, 2(a + b) = 2(5 + 4) = 18,$$

$$a(2 + c) = 5(2 + 3) = 25, \text{ and } c(2 + a) = 21.$$

The largest value is 35.

3. A: First, we determine $\frac{4}{3}$ of $\frac{33}{8}$. $\frac{4}{3} \times \frac{33}{8} = \frac{11}{2}$. Now, we find the missing number. Let n be the missing number. We have

$$n \div \frac{5}{6} = n \times \frac{6}{5} = \frac{11}{2}.$$

Therefore,

$$n = \frac{11}{2} \times \frac{5}{6} = \frac{55}{12}.$$

4. D: The numbers in the sequence are the following: 28; 196; 9604; 23,059,204. They are all multiples of 7 because dividing them each by 7 results in a whole number.

5. E: Let x be equal to the unknown value. Therefore, we have

$$146 + \frac{5}{6}x = x.$$

Subtract $\frac{5}{6}x$ from both sides of the equation to obtain

$$146 = \frac{1}{6}x.$$

Multiply both sides by 6 to find the solution $x = 876$.

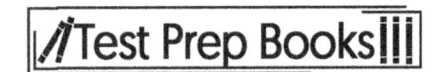

6. C: The first 8 positive multiples of 6 are 6, 12, 18, 24, 30, 36, 42, and 48. The average is equal to the sum of those digits divided by 8, which is $\frac{216}{8} = 27$. The median is equal to the average of the two middle values:

$$\frac{24 + 30}{2} = 27.$$

Therefore, the median minus the mean is actually 0.

7. E: Let q be the number of quarters and d be the number of dimes. Therefore, we have

$$q + d = 25$$

and

$$0.25q + 0.1d = 5.8.$$

We can solve this by substitution. Rewrite the first equation as $d = 25 - q$ and substitute into the second equation to obtain

$$0.25q + 0.1(25 - q) = 5.8.$$

This is equivalent to

$$0.25q + 2.5 - 0.1q = 5.8$$

or

$$0.15q = 3.3.$$

Divide through by 0.15 to obtain $q = 22$. Therefore, there are $d = 25 - 22 = 3$ dimes.

8. C: First, solve the corresponding equation $x^2 - 8 = 0$. It has two solutions: $x = \pm 2\sqrt{2}$. This breaks the number line into three possible regions that could be solutions to the inequality:

$$(-\infty, 2\sqrt{2}), (-2\sqrt{2}, 2\sqrt{2}), \text{ and } (2\sqrt{2}, \infty).$$

To determine whether each interval is a solution, we choose a value from that region and plug it in to see if it works. We choose

$$x = -10, 0, \text{ and } 10.$$

$(-10)^2 - 8 = 92$ does not work. $0^2 - 8 = -8$ does work. Finally, $(10)^2 - 8 = 92$ does not work. Therefore, $-2\sqrt{2} < x < 2\sqrt{2}$ is the correct option.

9. D: Because x is an odd number, the median of x consecutive integers is the number that falls in the middle when they are written in consecutive order. 160 is the middle number. There are $x - 1$ remaining values. Half of those values are less than or equal to 160, and half of those values are greater than or equal to 160. Since 160 is the middle number and they are consecutive integers, the values to the left of 160 are 159, 158, 157,... all the way to $160 - \frac{x-1}{2}$. Therefore, the smallest value is $160 - \frac{x-1}{2}$.

Answer Explanations #2

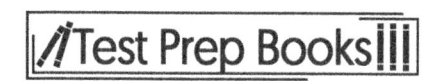

10. B: Let's say there are 100 pieces of inventory in the store. Therefore, there would be 20 pieces of produce in the store since 20% of the inventory consists of produce. 5% of the produce is apples, so there would be $(0.05)20 = 1$ apple in the store. The probability of selecting an apple is $\frac{1}{100} = 0.01 = 1\%$.

11. E: This problem involves finding the least common multiple (LCM) of 12, 8, and 7. We find the prime factorization of all three numbers: $12 = 2 \times 2 \times 3$, $8 = 2 \times 2 \times 2$, and 7 is already prime. We build the LCM by including each prime factor the greatest number of times it appears in any one factorization. Therefore, the LCM is $2 \times 2 \times 2 \times 3 \times 7 = 168$.

12. D: First, we equate the bases of the exponential expressions as:

$$5^{(a-16+2b)} = 5^{2(a+14+b)}.$$

This is because $25 = 5^2$. Because the bases are equal, we can equate the exponents. We now have the following equation:

$$a - 16 + 2b = 2(a + 14 + b)$$

Therefore,

$$a - 16 + 2b = 2a + 28 + 2b$$

The $2b$ terms cancel. Subtract a from both sides and subtract 28 from both sides to obtain

$$-44 = a.$$

13. A: This is a combination problem. There are 3 out of 8 possibilities for supervisors, which is equal to

$$C(8,3) = \frac{8!}{3!(8-3)!} = \frac{8 \times 7 \times 6}{3 \times 2 \times 1} = 56 \text{ possibilities.}$$

There are 2 out of 7 possibilities for managers, which is equal to

$$C(7,2) = \frac{7!}{2!(7-2)!} = \frac{7 \times 6}{2 \times 1} = 21 \text{ possibilities.}$$

Multiply these together to obtain $56 \times 21 = 1{,}176$ total possibilities.

14. D: This is a proportion problem. We set up the following proportion and solve:

$$\frac{25}{x} = \frac{y}{15}.$$

Cross-multiply to obtain $375 = xy$. Divide both sides by x to obtain $y = \frac{375}{x}$.

15. B: Choice *B* is correct. To find what 85% of 20 questions is, multiply 20 by .85:

$$20 \times .85 = 17 \text{ questions}$$

To find 80% of 25, multiply 25 by .80:

$$25 \times .8 = 20 \text{ questions}$$

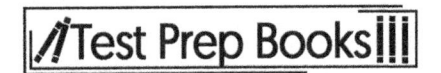

Student A got 17 questions correct and Student B got 20 questions. The difference between these is 3. If Student C took a test with 15 questions and got 3 of them incorrect, they got 12 questions correct. Student B answered 20 questions correctly, which is 8 more than Student C answered correctly.

16. E: If the average of all six numbers is 6, that means

$$\frac{a+b+c+d+e+x}{6} = 6$$

The sum of the first five numbers is 25, so this equation can be simplified to:

$$\frac{25+x}{6} = 6$$

Multiplying both sides by 6 produces a result of $25 + x = 36$. To solve for x, subtract 25 on both sides of the equation. The value of x, or the sixth number, is found to equal 11.

17. C: First, follow the order of operations in order to solve for the value to the right of the inequality sign. Solve the parentheses first, following the order of operations inside the parentheses as well. First, simplify the square roots:

$$(6 \times 4) - 3^2$$

Then, multiply inside the parentheses:

$$24 - 3^2$$

Next, simplify the exponents:

$$24 - 9$$

Finally, subtract to get 15.

This leaves the inequality $x + 5 < 15$. Isolate the x by subtracting 5 from both sides to get $x < 10$. The greatest integer than x can be is 9. The product of 3 and 9 is 27.

18. B: The first step is to make all exponents positive by moving the terms with negative exponents to the opposite side of the fraction. This expression becomes:

$$\frac{4b^3 b^2}{a^1 a^4} \times \frac{3a}{b}$$

Then the rules for exponents can be used to simplify. Multiplying the same bases means the exponents can be added. Dividing the same bases means the exponents are subtracted. Thus, after multiplying the exponents in the first fraction, the expression becomes:

$$\frac{4b^5}{a^5} \times \frac{3a}{b}$$

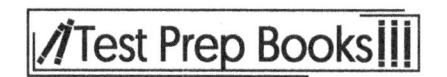

Therefore, we can first multiply to get:

$$\frac{12ab^5}{a^5b}$$

Then, simplifying yields:

$$12\frac{b^4}{a^4}$$

19. D: This problem can be solved by using unit conversion. The initial units are miles per minute. The final units need to be feet per second. Converting miles to feet uses the equivalence statement 1 mi = 5,280 ft. Converting minutes to seconds uses the equivalence statement 1 min = 60 s. Setting up the ratios to convert the units is shown in the following equation:

$$\frac{72 \text{ mi}}{90 \text{ min}} \times \frac{1 \text{ min}}{60 \text{ s}} \times \frac{5,280 \text{ ft}}{1 \text{ mi}} = \frac{380,160 \text{ ft}}{5,400 \text{ s}} = 70.4\frac{\text{ft}}{\text{s}}$$

The initial units cancel out, and the new units are left.

20. D: If $n = 2^2$, $n = 4$, and $m = 4^2 = 16$. This means that $m^n = 16^4$. But all the answer choices are written as powers of 2, so we can calculate:

$$16^4 = (2^4)^4 = 2^{4\times4} = 2^{16}$$

21. B: The given rate is equal to $\frac{18}{4} = \frac{9}{2}$ miles per hour. Choice A is equal to $\frac{4}{36} = \frac{1}{9}$, so this is not a correct option. Choice B is equal to $\frac{36}{8} = \frac{9}{2}$, so this is a correct option. Choice C is incorrect because it inaccurately simplifies $\frac{36}{8}$ to $\frac{9}{4}$, dividing the denominator by 2 instead of 4. Choice D simplifies to $\frac{180}{20} = 9$, and this is not equal to the given rate. Finally, Choice E is equal to $\frac{4}{9}$, which is an incorrect option. The only equivalent proportion is Choice B.

Verbal Reasoning

Reading Comprehension

1. B: The passage repeatedly mentions disputes over privatization, including inconclusive studies, scholars refuting the World Bank's statements about state-owned enterprises, and differences between free market advocates who want to "unleash" the private sector and the World Bank's more gradual approach. Thus, Choice B is the correct answer. Choice A is incorrect because "always" is too strong. The studies are inconclusive and have yielded conflicting results. Choice C is incorrect for similar reasons. Although the studies in this passage are criticized, it's too much to say economic studies in general are always subject to such criticism. The World Bank recommends that state-owned enterprises be privatized in accordance with commercial law, but that doesn't necessarily mean those enterprises violate commercial law, so Choice D is incorrect. Nowhere in the passage does it say the World Bank holds the power to intervene in economies; its statements are referred to as recommendations. Thus, Choice E is incorrect.

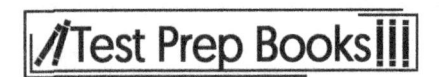

2. E: World Bank includes competition and corporate governance free of political interference in its five preconditions for successful privatization, making Choice *E* the correct answer. The passage states that state-owned enterprises have a "pervasive presence" in the global economy, making Choice *D* incorrect. The empirical research is inconclusive but, if anything, it leans toward the opposite of what's described in Choice *A*. Influences on the World Bank's policies and popular support for privatization are never mentioned in the passage; therefore, Choices *B* and *C* are incorrect.

3. C: The author's conclusion is that "SOEs are an entity to be considered and managed in the pursuit of stability." Thus, Choice C is the correct answer. The passage does not present a conclusion on whether privatization is an effective strategy. Choice *A* is not supported by the passage. Choices *B* and *D* are likely among the author's assumptions, but they are not conclusions. Choice *E* reflects the World Bank's position, but is not necessarily what the author believes.

4. C: The first sentence of the second paragraph states, "While spending more than other countries per capita on healthcare services, the United States spends less on average than do other nations on social services impacting social and behavioral determinants of health." Thus, Choice *A* is incorrect and *C* is correct. Choice *B* is incorrect because it reverses the United States' ratio. The author argues that America's lower life expectancy is due to lower spending on social services, not insufficient funding for health care, so Choice *D* is incorrect. Choice *E* is incorrect because the United States does fund interdisciplinary programs that include behavioral and social science, like the Clinical and Translational Science Awards.

5. C: The author repeatedly mentions how the United States neglects social services. According to the author, this is why the United States performs poorly on key health indicators despite spending more per capita on health care than any other country. In addition, the author argues that the Clinical and Translational Science Awards should hire more social and behavioral scientists. Thus, Choice *C* is the correct answer. Choices *A* and *D* are premises that support the conclusion, not the main thesis, so they are both incorrect. Choice *B* is incorrect because it's only providing background information about the Clinical and Translational Science Awards. The author never asserts that life expectancy is the most important healthcare indicator, and, even if that were true, it wouldn't be the main thesis. Thus, Choice *E* is incorrect.

6. C: Choice *C* is the correct answer because the passage emphasizes da Vinci's dissection of cadavers in order to show his dedication to making the most anatomically accurate art possible. Choice *A* is incorrect because the passage never compares da Vinci to his artist peers. Choice *B* is incorrect because the passage explains da Vinci's fascination with studying the human body to understand it better, not because he was obsessed with death. Choice *D* is incorrect because da Vinci's focus was on advancing his art, not medical research.

7. A: Choice *A* is the correct answer because the passage states that *sfumato* is a technique that blends colors to create soft transitions and an atmospheric quality. This was groundbreaking at the time. Choice *B* is incorrect because the popularity of the technique based on ease or difficulty is not discussed in the passage. Choice *C* is incorrect because the description of *sfumato* does not align with geometric art or art with many lines as it is about softness and blending. Choice *D* is incorrect because given the information that *sfumato* was considered *groundbreaking*, it can be inferred that more artists went on to use the technique rather than rejecting it.

Answer Explanations #2

8. C: Choice C is the correct answer because the example of a botanist studying the details of a leaf to later illustrate closely aligns with da Vinci studying the details of a human to later paint. Choice A is incorrect because da Vinci was drawn to creating his own highly specific paintings in their entirety rather than using generic environments. Choice B is incorrect because although the topic of studying something is similar, the agriculturalist is doing it in order to make an informed decision about something rather than to create something new. Choice D is incorrect because da Vinci did not seek to revive any traditional styles but rather wished to evolve his own techniques and create something new.

9. D: Choice D is the correct answer because the second paragraph focuses on how da Vinci's anatomical studies directly contributed to his accurate portrayal of the human body in art. He was able to create complex and expressive figure drawings that showed movement because of his studies of the tendons and muscles of cadavers. Choice A is incorrect because this passage does not mention da Vinci's philosophy and instead focuses on the actions he took to reach a goal. Choice B is incorrect because geometry and abstract art are not mentioned as they are not relevant to da Vinci's style. Choice C is incorrect because the focus is on da Vinci's use of science to enhance art rather than on any actual scientific accomplishments.

10. B: Choice B is the correct answer because the passage mentions that scientists are most interested in planets that may support life, which requires water and reasonable proximity to a star. Choice A is incorrect because a planet that is too close to a star would be extremely hot and uninhabitable. Choice C is incorrect because a gaseous planet with no oxygen would not be likely to support life. Choice D is incorrect because a planet with no atmosphere likely does not have water or oxygen to support life. The great distance from a star would also make it unlikely to support life.

11. B: Choice B is the correct answer because the transit method requires observation of star brightness fluctuations. It would not be effective in an area without stars. Choice A is incorrect because there is nothing in the passage to suggest that the transit method is outdated or that there are significantly better methods available. Choice C is incorrect because it misunderstands the use of biosignatures, which are used to detect signs of life on exoplanets, not to locate exoplanets themselves. Choice D is incorrect because an exoplanet was first discovered in 1992, but the first discovery of an exoplanet using the transit method occurred in 1999; therefore, the transit method cannot be the only possible method for finding exoplanets.

12. C: Choice C is the correct answer because the passage mentions various telescopes to highlight the need for advanced technology when attempting to find exoplanets. The telescopes mentioned are revolutionary, and mentioning them shows that finding exoplanets is a highly complex task that would not be possible without advanced space research technology. Choice A is incorrect because the passage never criticizes the current technology. Choice B is incorrect because the passage is not comparing the telescopes. Choice D is incorrect because the passage does not suggest that the telescopes are ineffective. In fact, it discusses how successful they have been in having been used to discover thousands of exoplanets.

13. D: Choice D is the correct answer because the last line of the passage expresses optimism about the future. The author appears to be hopeful that as technology advances, so will space discovery. Choice A is incorrect because there is no indication that the author is distrustful of the direction of space technology advancement or space exploration. Choice B is incorrect because the author's tone is positive rather than neutral, as evidenced by the last sentence. Choice C is incorrect because the author is not skeptical; they are presenting all of the information provided as factually sound.

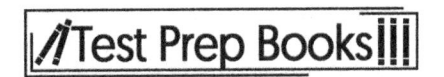

Critical Reasoning

14. C: Choice *A* is not present in the teacher's argument. There is no discussion of a common rule, so this cannot be the answer. Eliminate this choice.

Choice *B* is inaccurate. The teacher justifies his argument by pointing to the two highest achieving students in his class. It's not a perfect argument, but it's untrue to say that the argument is totally unjustified.

Choice *C* looks much more promising than the other options. The teacher's conclusion is that it's *always* the case that students can overcome parental indifference. He supports this notion by pointing to the two best students in a class of twenty people. The conclusion is too broad when considering the evidence. This is probably the answer, but look at the other choices to make sure.

Choice *D* does not correspond with anything in the teacher's argument. Although the teacher doesn't present any counter arguments, the existence of a competing theory is unclear. Eliminate this choice.

Choice *E* is clearly incorrect. The argument does not show any bias. Eliminate this choice.

Therefore, Choice *C* is the correct answer.

15. C: Choice *A* restates a premise and does not resolve the paradox. Whether Trent's SWAT team is the best police unit does not answer why unsolved crimes are increasing every year despite historic rates of crime solving. Eliminate this choice.

Choice *B* also does not resolve the paradox. It attempts to dismiss the increase in unsolved crimes by characterizing those crimes as petty drug offenses. Even if true, this does not resolve the paradox.

Choice *C* is a strong answer choice. If the raw number of crimes increases every year, then it makes sense that crimes are increasing despite the historic rates of crime solving. This explains the paradox. In questions involving percentages, always pay special attention to answer choices that involve raw numbers.

Choice *D* is irrelevant. The competence of the police department does not explain the paradox. Additionally, the police department is apparently not incompetent since it's solving a higher percentage of crimes than ever before in its history. Eliminate this choice.

Choice *E* is similar to Choice *B*. It attempts to dismiss the increasing number of unsolved crimes by claiming that the police are solving the most important crimes. This does not explain the paradox.

Therefore, Choice *C* is the correct answer.

16. C: Choice *A* definitely strengthens the argument by highlighting a benefit of an autocratic government. Eliminate this choice.

Choice *B* seems to strengthen the argument. This answer choice connects the start of the autocratic despot's reign with the start of economic growth. Eliminate this choice.

Choice *C* appears to weaken the argument. This answer choice provides an alternate explanation for the economic growth. According to Choice *C*, West Korea experienced economic growth as a result of the oil

Answer Explanations #2

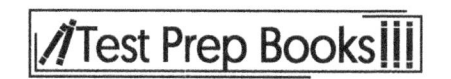

reserve. This hurts the argument's contention that West Korea's economy benefits from limiting civil liberties. This is a very strong answer choice.

Choice D clearly strengthens the argument. If political protest harms economic growth, then there's additional support for West Korea's curtailment of civil liberties. Eliminate this choice.

Choice E also strengthens the argument. The despot is able to devote all of his time to solving economic problems since there are no civil liberties. Eliminate this choice.

Therefore, Choice C is the correct answer.

17. E: Choice A is too extreme. The sociologist definitely believes that the abolition of marriage would harm society, but collapse goes too far. Eliminate this choice.

Choice B is tricky since the previous sentence references how children born out of wedlock are more likely to work at lower paying jobs. However, this answer choice also goes too far. According to the argument, unmarried people are less likely to be homeowners or save for retirement. But if marriage rates decline, it is not necessarily true that everyone would have less money. Eliminate this choice.

Choice C is tricky but also incorrect. Unmarried people are less likely to own homes. If marriage rates decline, fewer people would be homeowners. This is not the same as assuming that nobody would own homes. Eliminate this choice.

Choice D is irrelevant. The argument makes no reference to happiness. There is no way that such new information would logically complete the passage. Eliminate this choice.

Choice E looks much more promising than the other choices. If unmarried people are less likely to attend college and marriage rates decline, then it is reasonable to say that college attendance would probably decrease. Choice E also matches the argument's tone through the use of *probably*, unlike many of the other answer choices.

Therefore, Choice E is the correct answer.

18. B: Choice A is not a necessary assumption. This answer choice provides additional support to the argument, but it is not dependent on this fact. The test developers hope the test takers will mistake this for a strengthening question. Don't be fooled. Eliminate this choice.

Choice B looks very promising. Negate this answer choice to see if the argument falls apart: *Consumers' disposable income is NOT directly related to their ability to purchase goods and services.* This hurts the argument. If disposable income is unrelated to purchasing goods and services, then tax rates don't matter. Definitely keep this answer.

Choice C is irrelevant to the argument. The argument does not depend on consumers' preferences. Eliminate this choice.

Choice D is a strong answer choice. Negate this answer choice to see if the argument falls apart: *Increasing disposable income is NOT the only way to ensure economic growth.* The argument is definitely worse off, but it is not destroyed. Therefore, this is not a necessary assumption. Eliminate this choice.

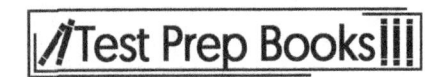

Choice *E* is irrelevant to the argument. The argument discusses how tax rates impact economic growth. It does not mention social welfare programs. Always be careful of new information, like the role social welfare programs play in this choice. Eliminate this choice.

Therefore, Choice *B* is the correct answer.

19. B: Choice *A* weakens one of the argument's premises. If big cats don't try to escape because they can't figure out their enclosures, then never attempting to escape is not a sign of intelligence. This definitely weakens the argument by negating one of its premises. Keep it for now.

Choice *B* looks extremely promising. This answer choice tells us that experts disagree that adjusting to captivity is a measure of intelligence. If big cats' adjustment to captivity does not correspond to intelligence, then the zookeeper's entire argument is flawed. This destroys the argument.

Choice *C* weakens the argument, but it's less powerful than Choice *B*. If bears share similarities with big cats, then there might be some doubt as to which animal is the smartest land mammal. This weakens the argument, but not as much as Choice *B*, which completely disrupts the argument's logic. Eliminate this choice.

Choice *D* actually strengthens the zookeeper's argument. The brain scans support the zookeeper's conclusion that big cats are the smartest land mammals. Eliminate this choice.

Choice *E* is a strong answer choice. If the zoo is devoting significantly more resources to caring for big cats, then the difference in resources could be the reason for their adaptability. However, Choice *B* spoils the argument's entire logical thrust. Eliminate Choice *E*.

Therefore, Choice *B* is the correct answer.

20. D: Choice *D* is the correct answer because it suggests that the residents' personal initiative to recycle earlier in the year could be a contributor to the yearly reduction in landfill waste. This would mean that the recycling campaign implemented later in the year is not the sole cause of the reduction in waste, and this would weaken the town council's argument. Choice *A* is incorrect because the campaign could still be the sole cause of the landfill waste reduction regardless of how many residents are aware of the campaign itself. This would not necessarily weaken the council's argument. Choice *B* is incorrect because it supports the council's argument by showing that their recycling initiatives are capable of being the sole reason that landfill waste has been reduced by 25 percent. Choice *C* is incorrect because the residents' increased motivation to recycle would point to the efficacy of the recycling bin initiative and thus to the efficacy of the campaign in general. That would strengthen the argument, not weaken it. Choice *E* is incorrect because an increase in the town's population does not directly relate to the council's recycling initiatives.

21. C: Choice *C* is correct because the survey strengthens Maria's argument that the decline in revenue is due to a lack of awareness among potential customers rather than to low customer satisfaction. If people nearby do not know about the shop, that indicates that its location is not highly visible and that there is insufficient advertising to inform people of the coffee shop's existence. Choice *A* is incorrect because mixed customer reviews do not affect Maria's argument. It is unclear what the mixed reviews are about and whether they relate to Maria's claims about poor location, a lack of advertising, and the in-shop experience. Choice *B* is incorrect because although the area's small businesses in general have had to reduce their advertising budgets, the passage does not indicate whether this reduction applies to

Answer Explanations #2

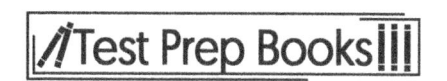

Maria's coffee shop specifically. The prices of rent and advertising neither strengthen nor weaken Maria's argument. Choice D is incorrect because knowing that competing coffee shops' sales are stable does not reveal why Maria's shop is struggling. Therefore, this statement does not strengthen her argument. Choice E is incorrect because while extensive repairs would cut into the shop's profits, that effect would not impact the sales revenue specifically. The repairs' impact on profits is also not directly related to any of the elements of Maria's argument—location, advertising, and customer satisfaction.

22. C: Choice C is the correct answer because a teen that is able to sleep adequately and get important tasks done is more likely to have improved mental health. It can also be inferred from this data that excessive social media use disrupts sleep patterns and negatively impacts performance on schoolwork, which indicates that it is detrimental to mental health. Choice A is incorrect because it indicates that academic work load may be a major factor in heightened stress levels, which contradicts Janet's argument. Choice B is incorrect because the survey does not specify whether the students are using their phones for social media during class time. Exam performance is also not a strong indicator of overall mental health. Choice D is incorrect because describing a positive effect of social media on students' engagement in educational material contradicts Janet's argument. Choice E is incorrect because the fact that some students share the stress of academic pressure online neither strengthens nor weakens Janet's argument that healthy social media habits could lead to better school performance.

23. C: Choice C is the correct answer because Joana's strong immune system and history of rarely falling ill would mean that she is not able to accurately conclude that the green tea is responsible for her lack of illness. Choice A is incorrect because substituting the green tea with another tea for a few days over the span of 6 months is unlikely to affect the experiment much. Choice B is incorrect because readers do not have insight into how long the friends have been drinking green tea or whether they are drinking it every day. Choice D is incorrect because the presence of antioxidants in other teas does not strengthen or weaken Joana's argument. The passage specifies that green tea is healthy due to its high antioxidant content; it is unclear whether the other types of tea have small or large amounts of antioxidants. Choice E is incorrect because although spending time outdoors may be benefiting Joana's health, not enough information is given—such as research data on decreased illness due to spending time outdoors—to justify attributing Joana's lack of illness to this change. Therefore, while this information may weaken Joana's argument to some degree, it would be less convincing than the information in Choice C.

Data Insights

Multi-Source Reasoning

1. C: The formula for compound annual growth rate in this situation would be $(650{,}000 \div 500{,}000)^{1/10} - 1$, which equals 2.7%.

2. Yes, No, No: For the first statement, refer to the data in Tab 1. Start by calculating the total increase in population between 2017 and 2023: 639,212 − 548,225 = 90,987. Next, calculate the number of years that have passed: 2023 − 2017 = 6 years. Lastly, divide the total increase in population by the number of years to get the average population increase: 90,987 ÷ 6 = 15,164.5, which means the answer to the first statement is *Yes*.

For the second statement, look in Tab 1 to find that the population in 2024 is 650,000. Since 95% of the population is employed, multiply 0.95 by 650,000 to find that 617,500 people in Austin are employed. Next, look at the information in Tab 2 to find that 25% of the employed population work in the manufacturing sector. Multiply 0.25 by 617,500 to get 154,375, which means the answer to the second statement is *No*.

For the third statement, begin by calculating what the population will be in 2025 if it is 2.5% higher than it was in 2024. 650,000 × (1 + 0.025) = 666,250. Then, calculate the 30% of this population that will make under $30,000: $666,250 × 0.3 = 199,875. Since this number is less than 200,000, the answer to this statement is *No*.

3. D: Tab 2 states that 60% of people in Austin work in the service industry, so the first statement is correct.

Tab 3 states that only 20% of people in Austin make over $70,000 per year, so the second statement is not accurate, eliminating Choices *A*, *C*, and *E*.

For the third statement, begin by calculating the unemployment rate: 100% − 95% = 5%. Calculate the number of people this would be by multiplying it by the population in 2024: 650,000 × 0.05 = 32,500 unemployed people in 2024. Next, calculate the population increase between 2023 and 2024: 650,000 − 639,212 = 10,788, and multiply this number by 3 to get 32,364 people. Since 32,500 is more than 32,364, this statement is correct.

For the fourth statement, look to Tab 1 to find the populations of Austin from 2018 to 2021, and calculate the total population for that time: 557,369 + 571,424 + 588,261 + 593,975 = 2,311,029. Next, calculate the number of years that passed during this time: 2021 − 2018 = 4 years. Finally, divide 2,311,029 by 4 to get the mean population of Austin from 2018 to 2021, which is 577,757.25. This means that the fourth statement is not accurate, eliminating Choice *B*.

Tab 3 states that 50% of people in Austin earn between $30,000 and $70,000 per year, so the fifth statement is accurate.

4. E: To begin to answer this question, start by taking the price of pants in 2024 ($59.99) and working backwards to 2023 using the percent price increases for each year. 2023: 59.99 ÷ (1 + 0.0514) = $57.06. Next, find the number of pants sold in 2023 if the number of pants sold in 2024 is 9,342 and sales have risen by 2.5% each year. 2023: 9,342 ÷ (1 + 0.025) = 9,114 pairs of pants sold. Multiply the price of pants in 2023 by the number of pairs sold to get $520,044.84 made from selling pants in 2023.

5. Yes, No, Yes: Approach the first statement by sorting the various garment prices for 2024 found in Tab 1 in ascending order and selecting the middle number ($40.25). Since this is the price of skirts, the statement is correct.

For the second statement, begin by calculating the price of shirts in 2021. 2023: 35.50 ÷ (1 + 0.0514) = $33.76. 2022: 33.76 ÷ (1 + 0.0459) = $32.28. 2021: 32.28 ÷ (1 + 0.0438) = $30.93. Then, find the number of shirts sold in 2021 if 10,211 were sold in 2024 and sales have gone up by 2.5% each year. 2023: 10,211 ÷ (1 + 0.025) = 9,961. 2022: 9,961 ÷ (1 + 0.025) = 9,718. 2021: 9,718 ÷ (1 + 0.025) = 9,480 shirts sold in 2021. 9,480 × 30.93 = $293,216.40. Since this is greater than $275,000, the statement is not accurate.

For the third statement, use the price of dresses in 2024 ($72.75) to calculate what the price will be in 2025 if prices go up by 6.5%. 72.75 × (1 + 0.065) = $77.48. Because this is greater than $75.50, the correct answer to this statement is *Yes*.

Answer Explanations #2

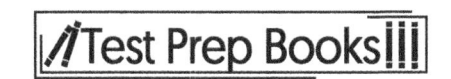

6. Yes, No, No: For the first statement, look at the prices for shorts ($25.99), skirts ($40.25), and dresses ($72.75) in 2024. The production cost for each item is 17.4% of the cost, so multiply each price by 17.4%. Shorts: 25.99 × 0.174 = $4.52. Skirts: 40.25 × 0.174 = $7.00. Dresses: 72.75 × 0.174 = $12.66. The combined cost of production per item for shorts and skirts is $11.52. Since $12.66 is more than $11.52, the statement is correct.

For the second statement, use the given percentages of price increases to calculate the mean increase from 2020 to 2023: (3.70 + 4.38 + 4.59) ÷ 3 = 4.22%, so this statement is not accurate.

For the third statement, begin by using the information from Tabs 1 and 2 to calculate the amount made from pants sales in 2024: 9,342 pants sold × $59.99 = $560,426.58 made from selling pants. Since 1.5% of the price of each item sold is donated to charity, take 1.5% of this number to get $8,406.40 donated to charity from pants sales in 2024. Therefore, the correct answer is *No*.

Graphics Interpretation

7. A, D: For the first sentence, look at the smallest and largest salaries displayed on the graph for the HR department. The range is approximately $34,000 to $65,000, so subtract $34,000 from $65,000 to get a value of $31,000 for the amount within the range.

For the second sentence, look to see the approximate maximum salary in sales ($81,000) and the minimum salary in maintenance ($31,000). Subtract to find the difference: $81,000 – $31,000 = $50,000.

8. B, C: The percentage of dads who feed their babies the peas less than 10 times per month is about 30%, and the percentage of moms who never feed their babies the peas is about 5%. 30 – 5 = 25%, so Choice *B* is correct.

For the second sentence, begin by finding the total percentage of moms who feed their babies the peas at least 10 times per month. Moms: for 10–20 times per month and >20 times per month, the sections of the chart combined look close to 75%. Next, do the same for the dads in the appropriate categories. Dads: approximately 12% (never) + approximately 30% (<10 times per month) = 42%. Then, subtract to find the difference between the two: 75 – 42 = 33%, which is close to Choice *C*, 30%.

9. A, C: Students with high numbers of study hours, such as Students 8 and 9, had consistently high grades. Students with low numbers of study hours had lower grades, and students with a medium number of study hours had grades in between. Thus, a strong correlation between hours spent studying and earning higher grades exists.

For the second sentence, look at the range for the grades for each student between the 2 semesters. Student 9 earned average grades of 88 and 95 for the two semesters. 95 – 88 = 7, which is the largest grade difference out of any of the students. Therefore, Choice *C* is the correct answer.

10. A, D: Begin answering for the first sentence by finding the percent increase for Site 2 between July and October: ([400 – 375] ÷ 375) × 100 = 6.67%. Next, do the same for Site 3 in the months of January through April: ([600 – 550] ÷ 550) × 100 = 9.09%. Then, subtract to find the difference between the two: 9.09 – 6.67 = 2.42%, so Site 2's increase was 2.42% less than Site 3's increase.

Answer Explanations #2

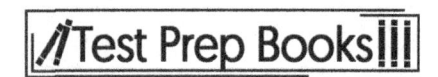

For the second sentence, start by finding the highest and lowest numbers for site traffic in the months of February through June. The lowest number is 100, and the highest number is 870. Then, subtract to find the difference between the two: 870 – 100 = 770.

Two-Part Analysis

11. Accounting is A and Marketing is C: There are 1,350 total business majors. Let a represent the number of accounting majors, and therefore the algebraic expression $3a$ can represent the number of marketing majors because there are 3 times as many accounting majors as marketing majors. There are 50 double majors. Therefore, we have the equation $1350 = a + 3a - 50$, which represents the total number of business majors. Subtracting the 50 represents any double-counting of double majors. Solving for a results in $a = 350$ the number of accounting majors. Therefore $3a = 1050$, the number of marketing majors. Therefore, the correct value for accounting is Choice *A*, 350, and the correct value for marketing is Choice *C*, 1,050.

12. Tended 3rd is D: The problem indicates that the tomatoes are tended to first and the carrots last. The basil must be in the fourth position, since it must go before the carrots. Since lettuce is never after basil, it can only be in the second or third position given the information so far. However, the cucumbers cannot go immediately after the lettuce. Thus, the proper order is tomatoes, cucumbers, lettuce, basil, and then carrots. Therefore, the third crop tended to each day would be lettuce, Choice *D*.

Tended 4th is A: See the explanation for question 1 for how to solve for the order to find that the fourth crop tended to each day is the basil, Choice *A*.

Table Analysis

13. No, Yes, No: Approach the first statement by listing the relevant North American quarterly sales, given the data provided. Q4 2021: $130.49, Q1 2022: $129.54, Q2 2022: $134.55. Then, calculate the growth rate for each quarter. For Q4 2021 through Q1 2022: ([129.54 – 130.49] ÷ 130.49) × 100 = –0.73%. For Q1 2022 through Q2 2022: ([134.55 – 129.54] ÷ 129.54) × 100 = 3.87%. Average these together to get the average growth rate for Q4 2021 through Q2 2022: (–0.73 + 3.87) ÷ 2 = 1.57%. 1.57% is less than 2.5%, so this statement is not accurate.

Begin solving the second statement by sorting the quarterly sales for Asia in ascending order. Since there are 13 numbers, select the middle number to find the median, which is $133.94 million. Therefore, the answer is *Yes*.

For the third statement, begin by listing the relevant quarterly sales in Europe, and then average these numbers together. Average Sales$_{Europe\ Q4\ 2022-Q3\ 2023}$ = (131.83 + 135.29 + 139.2 + 144.97) ÷ 4 = $137.82 million. Next, do the same for South America. Average Sales$_{South\ America\ Q4\ 2022-Q3\ 2023}$ = (100.88 + 104.62 + 110.93 + 121.95) ÷ 4 = $109.6 million. Since Europe's average sales for the specified time period were more than South America's average sales, the correct answer is *No*.

14. Yes, Yes, No: For the first statement, start by adding together the monthly corn production for each month to get the total for the year in 2023: 7.3 + 8.7 + 9.5 + 10.4 + 16.9 + 17.3 + 20.2 + 21.4 + 25.7 + 24.3 + 19.2 + 18.4 = 199.3 tons of corn in 2023. Next, calculate the total production of soybeans in 2023 the same way to get a total of 165.6 tons of soybeans produced in 2023. Account for the fact that production rates have risen by 1.25% each year to find what the soybean production was in 2021: 165.6

144

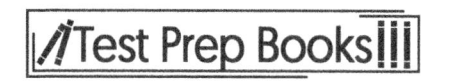

÷ (1 + 0.0125)² = 161.5 tons of soybeans in 2021. Since 199.3 is greater than 162.5, the first statement is accurate.

For the second statement, begin by listing the production values for soybeans in ascending order and averaging the two middle values to get the median. Median = (12.2 + 12.3) ÷ 2 = 12.25. Double this number to get 24.5. Finally, compare this number to the corn production in October (24.3). Since 24.3 is less than 24.5, the correct answer is *Yes*.

Begin to address the third statement by adding together the amount of tobacco produced each month between June and December and finding the average of these numbers: 8.1 + 9.8 + 11.4 + 13.1 + 12.6 + 10.2 + 8.6 = 73.8 ÷ 7 = 10.54 tons. Next, add together the production values for rice for the months of January through July to get the total amount produced during that time: 8.4 + 6.2 + 7.9 + 8.7 + 9.5 + 12.2 + 13.1 = 66 tons of rice. Finally, check to see if the average amount of tobacco (10.54 tons) was 55.46 tons more than the amount of rice (66 tons). Since 10.54 is 55.46 *less* than 66, the answer to this statement is *No*.

15. No, No, No: Approach the first statement by calculating the total rainfall for all of the cities for the year to get a total of 415.7 inches. Then calculate 30% of this: 415.7 × 0.3 = 124.71 inches. Compare this to Mumbai's rainfall in 2023 (94.1 inches). Since 94.1 is less than 124.71, the statement is not accurate.

For the second statement, start by calculating the ratio of rainfall to rainy days in London in 2023. Rainfall was 64.4 inches, and there were 145 rainy days. Therefore, the ratio for London is 64.4:145 (0.4441). Next, do the same for Paris. Rainfall was 27.5 inches, and the city had 97 rainy days. The ratio for Paris is 27.5:97 (0.2835). Finally, check to see if the ratio for London was at least 65% more: 0.2835 × 1.65 = 0.4678. Since the ratio for London (0.4441) is less than 65% more than the ratio for Paris (0.4678), the correct answer is *No*.

For the third statement, identify the city with the third highest number of rainy days: New York. Then, find which city has the third highest amount of rainfall: São Paulo. This means that the third statement is not accurate.

Data Sufficiency

16. B: Statement 1 only provides information about Portfolio A and no information about Portfolio B, so it is not sufficient. Statement 2 says that Portfolio B has a return of 2.3% more than twice that of Portfolio A, which means that A shows a smaller annual return. Therefore, Statement 2 is sufficient alone.

17. E: Statement 1 provides enough information to calculate the efficiency of Machine A, but it does not give us any information about Machine B, so it is not sufficient. Statement 2 provides the energy consumed by Machine B but not the number of units produced, so it does not have enough information to calculate its efficiency. Therefore, both statements together are not sufficient.

18. A: Statement (1) states that Katie can finish the story in 4 hours, which means that Serena can finish the story in 8 hours because Katie is twice as fast as Serena. Because both of these quantities create rates, together they can finish one story in:

$$\frac{1}{4} + \frac{1}{8} = \frac{2}{8} + \frac{1}{8} = \frac{3}{8}$$

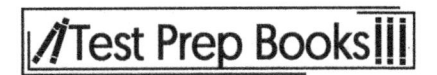

Dividing 8 by 3 shows that together they can finish the story in $2\frac{2}{3}$ hours. Therefore (1) is sufficient. Statement (2) is insufficient because we do not know how long the story is that they need to complete.

19. D: Statement (1) is sufficient. Because there is a 25% profit on each box, oatmeal is sold for:

$$\$2 + 0.25 \times \$2 = \$2 + \$0.50 = \$2.50$$

Statement (2) is also sufficient. Because your selling price is 80% of your purchase price, $\$2 = 0.8 \times p$, where p is the purchase price. Therefore, $p = \frac{\$2}{.8} = \$2.50$. Both statements (1) and (2) are sufficient individually.

20. E: Statement (1) is not sufficient. If the mean is 3, then the sum of values is 21. If the median is 3, the middle of the values is 3. Neither one answers the question. Statement (2) is not sufficient. Knowing how many times the mode appears does not help us determine whether the median is less than the mode.

Index

Addition, 10, 12, 17
Articles, 49
Average, 16, 27, 28, 40, 60, 108, 110, 111, 134, 136
Base, 12, 23, 49
Bias, 30, 36, 138
Cancel, 11, 15
Cause and Effect, 31, 70, 96
Common Denominator, 10, 11, 16
Comparison-Contrast, 30, 31
Complex Sentence, 31
Conclusion, 33, 41, 42, 53, 114, 136, 138, 140
Counter-Argument, 33
Decimal Number, 12, 13
Decimal Place, 12, 13
Decimal Point, 12, 13, 21
Decimal System, 12
Denominator, 10, 11, 13, 14, 19, 23
Dependent, 139
Descriptive, 31
Difference, 10, 11, 17, 21, 57, 59, 60, 89, 140
Divide Into One Another, 11
Dividend, 11, 13
Division, 11, 13, 17
Divisor, 11, 13
Essential, 39, 41
Estimation, 12, 15
Examples, 16, 19, 21, 22, 29, 30, 32, 33
Explanation, 30, 95, 96, 138
Expository, 30
Fact, 36, 41, 139
First-Person Point of View, 31
Flashback, 34
Generalization, 70
Image, 31
Improper Fraction, 11
Inference, 34
Introduction, 30, 32
Inversely Proportional, 15
Jargon, 30
Logical Fallacy, 36
Main, 30, 31, 32, 33, 39, 41, 111, 136
Mean, 16, 31, 130, 135, 146
Mixed Number, 11

Multiplication, 10, 13, 17
Narrative, 29
Numerator, 10, 11, 19, 23
Ordinary Average, 16
Paraphrasing, 32, 33
Percent, 13, 14, 15, 16, 21, 89
Persuasive, 29, 30
Phrase, 13
Plane, 26
Point of View, 31, 32
Points, 26, 33
Positive, 23, 48
Predictions, 34
Problem-Solution, 31
Product, 10, 48, 49, 50
Proper Fraction, 11
Proportional, 15
Pythagorean Formula, 26
Quotient, 11, 17, 53
Ratio, 15, 20, 110, 111, 136
Reciprocal, 11
Rectangle, 15
Repeating, 12
Rounding, 15
Second-Person Point of View, 32
Sequence, 30, 34
Similar, 19, 42, 48, 52, 135, 138
Simplified, 11, 14, 22, 23, 134
Square, 15, 21
Subject, 31, 32, 35, 36, 37, 110, 135
Subtraction, 10, 13, 17
Sum, 10, 16, 17, 108, 134, 146
Summarizing, 33
Supporting Details, 32, 33
Technical, 29, 30
Terminating, 12
Textual Evidence, 33
Thesis Statement, 32
Third-Person Limited, 32
Third-Person Objective, 32
Third-Person Omniscient, 32
Third-Person Point of View, 31
Tone, 37
Topic, 30, 32, 35, 37, 49

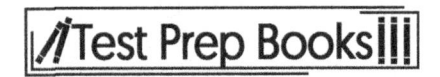

Translation, 111
Weighted Average, 16

Weighted Mean, 16

Dear GMAT Focus Edition Test Taker,

Thank you for purchasing this study guide for your GMAT Focus Edition exam. We hope that we exceeded your expectations.

Our goal in creating this study guide was to cover all of the topics that you will see on the test. We also strove to make our practice questions as similar as possible to what you will encounter on test day. With that being said, if you found something that you feel was not up to your standards, please send us an email and let us know.

We would also like to let you know about other books in our catalog that may interest you.

GRE

This can be found on Amazon: amazon.com/dp/B0CJLCZVCS

MCAT

amazon.com/dp/1637754159

We have study guides in a wide variety of fields. If the one you are looking for isn't listed above, then try searching for it on Amazon or send us an email.

Thanks Again and Happy Testing!
Product Development Team
info@studyguideteam.com

FREE Test Taking Tips Video/DVD Offer

To better serve you, we created videos covering test taking tips that we want to give you for FREE. **These videos cover world-class tips that will help you succeed on your test.**

We just ask that you send us feedback about this product. Please let us know what you thought about it—whether good, bad, or indifferent.

To get your **FREE videos**, you can use the QR code below or email freevideos@studyguideteam.com with "Free Videos" in the subject line and the following information in the body of the email:

   a. The title of your product

   b. Your product rating on a scale of 1-5, with 5 being the highest

   c. Your feedback about the product

If you have any questions or concerns, please don't hesitate to contact us at info@studyguideteam.com.

Thank you!

Made in the USA
Coppell, TX
16 February 2025